"*Be Healed and Stay Healed* is a
personal journey into learning
This book is full of faith-igniting testimonies that fuel our love
for God and create in us a hunger to see greater breakthroughs
in our lives. Read this book with expectation, as the author
activates your faith to see the Kingdom come as promised."

Bill Johnson, senior pastor,
Bethel Church, Redding, California

"This book is so very real and honest. We all can easily identify
with Ed on his journey in learning God's ways in healing. In
this very effective teaching approach, anyone can actually learn
to move from 'desiring earnestly the best gifts' to operating
confidently in the joy and power of our Lord Jesus to see real
results—all to God's glory. This is my kind of 'healing book'!"

Jon Mark Ruthven, professor emeritus
of theology, Regent University; doctor of ministry
mentor, United Theological Seminary

"*Be Healed and Stay Healed* is a book I am confident to recommend. Ed weaves powerful truths through personal testimonies
of victories and failures in his pursuit of God's healing power.
In addition, he addresses issues from which others often shy
away. Everyone who reads this book will feel encouraged and
inspired to heal the sick."

Dr. Tom Jones, executive director,
Global Awakening Ministries

"Ed Rocha's stories of healing and breakthrough will stir your
heart to believe for more. *Be Healed and Stay Healed* is a must-
read if you long to be a part of seeing cities saved, nations
transformed and those around you marked by the presence of
God. With great humility and wisdom, Ed calls us to step out
of our comfort zones and into all God has for us."

Banning Liebscher, director,
Jesus Culture

"Ed Rocha's *Be Healed and Stay Healed* is a book I highly recommend. Ed not only gives you keys to healings and miracles but also shares some of the most astounding testimonies of healings and miracles I have ever heard. This book will definitely challenge and motivate you to pursue the power of God to be healed yourself and to heal the sick. I love it when I read a book that leads me to an encounter with God."

Cal Pierce, director,
Healing Rooms Ministries

"*Be Healed and Stay Healed* is a practical unfolding of what Ed Rocha has witnessed firsthand. Each chapter offers profound wisdom that comes from a lifetime of walking supernaturally with the Lord. Ed combines sound biblical truths and insights with honest, vulnerable testimonies that will release great faith in your heart. If you desire to see healings, signs and wonders, I highly recommend that you read *Be Healed and Stay Healed* from cover to cover."

Georgian Banov, president and co-founder,
Global Celebration

"Loved the book for three reasons: First, Ed is full of faith, yet humble, delightful and approachable. Second, the book is simple to read and comprehend. Third, it raises people's faith level so they can be healed and stay healed, and so they also can heal others."

Happy Leman, senior pastor,
The Vineyard Church of Central Illinois

BE
HEALED
and
STAY
HEALED

BE HEALED
and
STAY HEALED

Practical Tools, Key Principles,
Proven Prayers, Faith-Building Testimonies

ED ROCHA

Chosen

a division of Baker Publishing Group
Minneapolis, Minnesota

Published by Chosen Books
11400 Hampshire Avenue South
Bloomington, Minnesota 55438
www.chosenbooks.com

Chosen Books is a division of
Baker Publishing Group, Grand Rapids, Michigan

Printed in the United States of America

ISBN 978-0-8007-9781-2

Library of Congress Control Number: 2015952329

The names and certain identifying details of some individuals have been changed in order to protect their privacy.

Unless otherwise indicated, Scripture quotations are from the Holy Bible, New International Version®. NIV®. Copyright © 1973, 1978, 1984, 2011 by Biblica, Inc.™ Used by permission of Zondervan. All rights reserved worldwide. www.zondervan.com

Scripture quotations identified ESV are from The Holy Bible, English Standard Version® (ESV®), copyright © 2001 by Crossway, a publishing ministry of Good News Publishers. Used by permission. All rights reserved. ESV Text Edition: 2007

Scripture quotations identified NASB are from the New American Standard Bible®, copyright © 1960, 1962, 1963, 1968, 1971, 1972, 1973, 1975, 1977, 1995 by The Lockman Foundation. Used by permission.

Scripture quotations identified NKJV are from the New King James Version. Copyright © 1982 by Thomas Nelson, Inc. Used by permission. All rights reserved.

Scripture quotations identified NLT are from the *Holy Bible*, New Living Translation, copyright © 1996, 2004, 2007 by Tyndale House Foundation. Used by permission of Tyndale House Publishers, Inc., Carol Stream, Illinois 60188. All rights reserved.

Scripture quotations identified NRSV are from the New Revised Standard Version of the Bible, copyright © 1989, by the Division of Christian Education of the National Council of the Churches of Christ in the United States of America. Used by permission. All rights reserved.

Scripture quotations identified WEB are from the World English Bible.

Cover design by Gearbox

16 17 18 19 20 21 22   7 6 5 4 3 2 1

I want to dedicate this book to my wife, Danieli,
the greatest love of my life, my best friend and life partner,
for all her support and for bringing the *How* to my *What*.

Contents

Foreword

by Randy Clark

Ed Rocha's *Be Healed and Stay Healed* is a wonderful read, filled with powerful stories of what the "I Am" is still doing in the world today regarding signs and wonders. This is not a book about the "I Was" or the "I Will Be," where the powerful acts of God are relegated to the past or put off until the millennial reign. Ed is a masterful storyteller who recounts the testimonies of those people he personally has seen being healed in our day.

I have known Ed Rocha for almost ten years. He has traveled with me all over Brazil and has been with me in the United States. He has served as my interpreter, and he has received a strong impartation for ministry in the supernatural. He also moves prophetically in times of impartation. His powerful prophetic word to Rev. Marcelo Casagrande about his healing crusades throughout all of Latin America was fulfilled to the letter within a year.

Be Healed and Stay Healed is not a report from secondary sources. It is a firsthand account of what Ed has experienced.

I can verify most of these reports myself because I was there when many of them occurred. I saw many of these miracles Ed tells about happen, and I know them to be true. Reading these reports, the testimonies of what Jesus has done, resulted in increasing my faith.

I believe these stories will challenge anyone who has a skeptical or cynical predisposition to unbelief. Such stories challenged my enlightenment training—the worldview that nothing supernatural is possible, and the idea that to believe in the supernatural is superstitious, not based on scientific investigation. Due to experiencing miracles, I had to give up my enlightenment training early on in my theological training! I believe that is the kind of effect Ed's stories will have.

I recommend *Be Healed and Stay Healed* to you as a book. I recommend *Be Healed and Stay Healed* to you as an experience of God's empowering presence. I am proud to have Ed Rocha as my spiritual son, and his wife, Dani, as my spiritual daughter. Ed is also one of my few associate evangelists at Global Awakening Ministries, and I recommend his ministry to you.

Go ahead—take a look into a world that may be very different from your worldview and experience. I challenge you with the same words the Holy Spirit challenged me with: "Do not be an experience-based preacher who only preaches what he has experienced. Do not lower My Word to the level of your experience, but let your experience rise to the level of My Word."

I want to encourage you to believe that Jesus is the same today as He was when He walked on the earth, except that now He lives in and through us.

—Dr. Randy Clark, founder, Global Awakening Ministries

Acknowledgments

I want to thank Dr. Randy Clark, my mentor and spiritual father, for tucking me under his wing and helping me in this incredible journey of finding out who I am in Christ. I also want to thank him for awakening me to my destiny.

Many thanks to my friend Dr. Jon Ruthven, whose insight and supervision were instrumental in helping keep this book theologically sound.

I also want to thank my friend Susan Fleming for encouraging me to write when nobody knew that writing was on my heart.

Many thanks to Tracy Shuman for helping me with the first edits of this project.

I would also like to thank the Red Arrow Media family, especially Jennifer Westbrook, for the excellent editorial work.

A Word Before

Nothing Stronger Than the Cross

Since I started my journey into the healing ministry almost ten years ago, I have seen all sorts of healings take place. I have seen everything from headaches to cancer disappear. The blind have seen, the deaf have heard, the lame have walked and the dead have even been raised. I have also seen that there is a sad reality in the healing ministry: Not everyone who is prayed for gets healed, and not everyone who gets healed stays healed. I wrote this book to tackle these issues because I fully believe that nothing is stronger than the power of the cross—not sin, sickness or even death.

God wants everyone to be healed and stay healed. When we turn our affections toward God and connect our hearts to His, we become catalysts of His presence and His miracle-working power. When we engage with God, we become Kingdom partners, seeking to establish His will on the earth.

God wants you filled with His miracle-working power so that you can carry it with you wherever you go. He wants to empower you to push darkness away as you shine forth His light and claim territory for our King.

If you picked up this book, chances are that you believe strongly in the supernatural power of God for healing and want to experience it. You may need healing yourself, or you may want to participate in the healing ministry for others who are afflicted. Either way, physical healing is one of God's promises for us, His children. Healing is our inheritance. God not only wants to answer your prayers so that you can be healed and stay healed; He also wants to use you as an ambassador for Jesus.

Every Christian is called to build the Kingdom of God and glorify the name of Jesus through the operation of signs, wonders, healings and miracles. Jesus commanded us to do these things. Understanding physical healing is essential in order to see His good and perfect will fulfilled in our lives. As children of God, we ought to be prepared for the healing ministry. We ought to know how to use the spiritual tools and weapons God has provided to effectively destroy the works of the devil in our lives and in the lives of those around us.

In *Be Healed and Stay Healed*, I will equip you with some key principles, teaching, prayers and testimonies that are intended to stir up your faith and increase your anointing. I hope the stories and spiritual tools I share in this book will bless and inspire you. I pray that you will experience the power of God and live out the truth of the Gospel in a new dimension because of what you read here. May God continue to guide you by His Spirit on this beautiful, exciting adventure of exploring His supernatural power. May He take you to a new level where heaven meets earth and all things are possible!

PART ONE

The Testimony of Jesus

1

The Deaf Hear

Be Motivated by Love

They brought unto him a deaf man. . . . Then looking up to
heaven, he sighed and said to him, "Ephphatha," that is, "Be
opened." And immediately his ears were opened.

Mark 7:32–35 NRSV

Miracles are humanly impossible. Scientists and others in the
medical field can do nothing to make a deaf ear instantly and
naturally hear. There have been incredible improvements in
audiology, especially in the area of hearing implants and stem
cell regeneration. Stanford University's Otolaryngology Depart-
ment in California is developing new inner ear hair cells with
stem cell technology and successfully producing stem cells that
behave like hair cells. If they can generate these hair cells in
the millions, they will be much closer to curing deafness in
the future.[1]

Even with technological advancements and groundbreaking discoveries like this, however, science deals with the effects of hearing loss, not the cause. Doctors cannot reverse inner ear damage, nor can they cause a totally deaf person, especially one deaf from birth, to hear . . . but God can.

That is where we come in as believers. "And he sent them out to proclaim the kingdom of God and to heal" (Luke 9:2 NRSV). Jesus sent out His disciples with miracle-working power, and He still is sending us out the same way today.

"Ephphatha!"

The first time I prayed for a deaf person, I did everything wrong. I was with Randy Clark, leader and founder of Global Awakening, in a crusade in São Paulo, Brazil, almost ten years ago. I had just met Randy and was translating for him. I had never seen anyone flow in the anointing the way he did. His prayers were simple, yet so profound and effective. Watching God's power flow through him to heal the sick made me hunger to have that kind of anointing flowing through my life.

When it was time to pray for the sick, Randy said, "Okay now, all those who want physical healing come to the front, and my team and I will stand here in front of the platform and pray for you. Come! Come now!"

Hundreds of people came to the front, and for the first time I stood with Randy and the team to pray for people. When I saw the multitude coming forward to receive prayer, I prayed to the Lord under my breath, *Father, You know I'm new to this, so please send me an easy one.*

The very first person who came to me for prayer was a young man.

"What would you like prayer for?" I asked him.

20

He answered with scrambled and muffled, indistinct sounds and funny hand gestures.

Oh, no, I thought, *not a deaf-mute person, Lord. When I said "easy," I meant easy for me, not for You. I meant a headache or a bellyache.* (When you tell God, "Send me an easy one," make sure you mention that it should be easy according to your standards, not His!)

A young lady came up from behind him and said, "This is my brother. He's been deaf from birth. Could you please pray for him to be healed?"

I replied, "Deaf? Oh, no, no . . ." I waved both hands in total disapproval. "You should take him to Randy or one of the Americans; I'm new to this. I'm trying to heal headaches here."

The young lady said, "No, their lines are too long, and we have to go home. You pray." The deaf man smiled.

I wanted to cry. I had no idea what to do. I was just the translator, not a speaker or even a team member. But I had been watching Randy pray and heal many people, so I decided I would do what I saw him doing. As I started to pray, I copied Randy's style—the way he placed his hands on the sick, the soft tone of his voice and the nice, encouraging words he said.

I prayed Randy's classic healing prayer: "Come, Holy Spirit." Then after a minute or two I said to the young man's sister, "Ask him if he feels any difference."

His sister asked him in sign language and then told me, "No, not at all."

That was not very encouraging, but I had seen Randy pray a few times for people before anything happened, so I gave it another try.

"Tell him I'm going to pray again," I said. This time, I prayed with a little more emphasis on the words, speaking a little more loudly. I prayed for another minute or two and then stopped and asked his sister to ask him if he was any better.

The sister asked, and the deaf-mute boy shook his head and spoke to her in sign language.

"No, still nothing," the sister told me.

I started feeling upset and frustrated. A lot of people were gathering around me, watching my every move, just as I would do to Randy. Only in this case nothing was happening—no healing at all.

"Let me try again," I said to the sister as I folded up my sleeves. This time I prayed every prayer I could think of. My Pentecostal background kicked in, and I started to pray like the African-American missionary preachers I had heard as a teenager. Suddenly, my monosyllabic words had three or four syllables: "You fa-a-oul spirit of deafness-uh, come-oughtaah!"

The sister went through the translating drill again and told me, "Still nothing."

That went on for about fifteen or twenty minutes. I prayed all the prayers I could think of. At one point I even licked my fingers, stuck them in the boy's ears and shouted, *"Ephphatha! Ephphatha! Ephphatha!"* (the Aramaic word meaning "be opened" that Jesus used when He healed a deaf boy in Mark 7:34).

The more I shouted, the more people gathered around me to watch. Yet nothing happened. I was making such a fool of myself. This was summertime in Brazil, and there were hundreds of people inside that little building without air conditioning. I was soaked in sweat, with all these people staring at me, waiting to see the boy healed.

I felt so much pressure. I kept thinking, *This is the devil trying to make a fool out of me.* So I grabbed the boy by the collar and shouted with all the power in my lungs, "Deaf-and-dumb spirit, come out!"

I think a vein popped in my neck. If there were any demons afflicting him, I like to imagine that they must have surely been hanging on for dear life as I shouted at the boy's ear the way a T. rex would scream at its prey.

The sister did the asking drill again, but there was still nothing.

At this point I was sweaty, tired, discouraged, desperate and lost. The deaf boy must have noticed that I had no idea what I was doing, because he finally shrugged his shoulders and said something to his sister in sign language.

The sister looked at me and said, "He said that he's tired, and it's late. We've got to go home. Thanks for trying."

They waved good-bye with a smile and left. I had no line anymore; nobody stayed for prayer. The people who had gathered around me looked me over from head to toe before turning on their heels and leaving.

On the way to the airport the next morning, everyone on the team was so excited, telling stories and sharing healing testimonies. Everyone was happy . . . everyone but me. I was miserable. For three days after I returned home, I moped. Usually I had my time alone with God every day, but after that night I did not want to pray, not for a while. I did not know it at the time, but I was about to learn a very important lesson.

Motives

I was mad at God. Finally, after three days of silence, I went to my room and prayed, *God, why did You let me look like a fool in front of all those people? Why didn't You heal that boy?* I never had God answer me more quickly, as if He had been waiting for me to ask.

What was his name? I heard the Holy Spirit ask in my spirit's ear.

What? I asked.

You heard Me. God did not sound very happy. *What was the deaf boy's name?*

I don't know, I answered.

And do you know why you don't know? the Father asked.

No, I don't know why I don't know, but I have a feeling You're going to tell me.

You don't know because you didn't care. You didn't want him to be healed; you wanted you to heal him. You didn't pray for him because you loved him; you wanted him to be healed so that you could look good in front of those people.

Those words hit me like a punch in the face. I immediately fell to my knees, weeping before the Lord, convicted of my sin. His words were true, and I knew it. He knew that I did not have His love in my heart (see John 5:42). I did not care at all about that boy's life. All I wanted at that point was to be the man of power for the hour.

With tears running down my face, I prayed, *O God, please change me. Clean my heart. I don't want to be like that anymore. I don't want to be selfish and carnal.*

I was not angry with God anymore. As I wailed, rocking back and forth on that cold tile floor wet with my tears, I repented of my sin and saw a vision of a hand in front of me. I knew it was the Lord's hand. The hand went through my rib cage, grabbed something in my heart and pulled it out. When I looked at it, I was disgusted. It looked like a big lump of filthy tar, and it smelled terrible.

As the Lord's hand pulled out that black, dripping phlegm from my heart, I asked Him, still sobbing, *O Lord, what is that?*

That's anger, bitterness, hatred and selfishness, He answered.

Take it away from me, Father. Please cleanse my heart from all of it.

The hand of the Lord went in again three times. I felt so tremendously empty after that, and I cried out for His love and mercy to fill me up. After being cleansed from all that filth, I continued to weep as wave after wave of liquid love filled my heart.

The Lord asked me, *Do you feel My love? I am love.* His beautiful voice echoed inside me. *Without Me, you can do nothing.* Then the truth dawned on me. Jesus said, "Apart from me you can do nothing" (John 15:5). Jesus is God, and God is love. If we do not have love in our hearts, then we are on our own, and believe me, that is a sad, lonely and scary place to be. Only with love will we be able to heal the sick; only motivated by love will we be able to perform miracles; only overflowing with love and compassion will we attract the One who releases power to heal. Apart from Him we can do nothing. In order to receive the healing power and anointing of God for your personal healing or the healing of others, you first must be filled with His love. He does not give His power to anyone except the ones who love Him.

Take Simon from the book of Acts, for example. A sorcerer in Samaria, Simon amazed everyone from that region, convincing people from both high and low levels of society that he possessed great power from God. When Simon saw Philip perform great signs and miracles in the name of Jesus, he believed the message and was baptized. Then when Peter and John came to Samaria, they prayed for the new converts to receive the Holy Spirit. Interested in the demonstration of power he was witnessing, Simon wanted that same power:

> When Simon saw that the Spirit was given at the laying on of the apostles' hands, he offered them money and said, "Give me also this ability so that everyone on whom I lay my hands may receive the Holy Spirit."
> Peter answered: "May your money perish with you, because you thought you could buy the gift of God with money! You have no part or share in this ministry, because your heart is not right before God. Repent of this wickedness and pray to

the Lord in the hope that he may forgive you for having such a thought in your heart."

Acts 8:18–22

Simon repented and asked for forgiveness. He was a new convert and did not know that the power of God could not be purchased. He did not understand that God is not for sale. He also did not understand that God is not moved by what we can do, so much as by who we can become.

Set Up by God

After the Lord spoke to me that day about being motivated by and dependent on love, I never again allowed those evil feelings He had removed with His hand to find a home in my heart. Nevertheless, the experience I had where the deaf boy was unhealed was traumatic for me, and I stopped trying to pray for the sick. Three years went by, and I continued to travel with Randy and translate for him in Brazil. During those three years, God was doing a deep work in my heart, breaking the foundation of wrong teachings about healing and giving me deeper revelations about His love, mercy and undeserved grace. I had been growing in my relationship with the Father, but I still felt uncomfortable about praying for anyone for healing. I was afraid I would "miss it" again.

That is, until Father God set me up. I was with Randy at another crusade in Uberlândia, Brazil, attended by over four thousand people. Many wonderful miracles happened in that crusade. Hundreds of people were healed of all sorts of illnesses, and thousands were baptized in the Holy Spirit. I saw hundreds of people getting healed with my own eyes, but I did not dare pray for anyone. Then one of the team members from America, a young man called Rob, approached me and asked if I could help him by translating while he prayed for a guy outside the building. I agreed to help and followed him to an open area outside.

Rob walked up to a man and told me, "Find out what he needs healing for."

I asked him, and he replied, "I'm deaf."

"What percentage of your hearing have you lost?" I asked.

"I didn't lose it. I was born completely deaf."

I looked at him with a confused expression on my face and asked, "If you are deaf, how come you can understand and answer me?"

He gave me a big, bright smile and said, "I can read lips."

I told Rob the man's condition, and before he began to pray, he turned to me and said, "Ed, I feel in my spirit that the Father wants *you* to pray for this one."

"What? Who? Me?" I stuttered.

"Yes, you," he said, firm as a rock. "I feel that the Father is saying you're supposed to pray for him."

"No, Rob," I said, trying to wipe out a nervous smile. "I'm just a translator, okay? You pray, and I'll translate for you."

Rob insisted, "I really feel like the Father wants you to pray for this guy, Ed."

Suddenly, I knew he was right. I felt the Holy Spirit tell me that the Father wanted me to pray for this man. As soon as I agreed in my spirit, the memory of the deaf boy from three years before flashed in my mind. The image of me screaming helplessly at the boy while everyone watched, the pain of the defeat when no healing manifested, the anguish of the vision when that hand had pulled the tar out of my chest—they all combined to cause me to panic. I looked at Rob, and he nodded his head at me, signaling that it was time for me to pray.

I looked up to the stars and said, *Okay, Father, I guess I've been running from this for too long.* I turned to the deaf man and said, "Give me your hands."

As soon as he placed his hands on mine, I remembered the most valuable lesson the Lord had ever taught me, so I asked for his name.

"Paul," he answered with a big smile.

"Okay, Paul," I said, speaking slowly and clearly to make sure he could read my lips correctly, "keep your eyes open so you can read my lips. As long as I'm touching you, I'm praying for you, even if I don't say anything, okay?"

"Okay," he answered with his peculiar lisp.

I looked up to the stars and prayed silently, *Father, I know that apart from You I can do nothing. And to be honest with You, I don't love this guy. How could I? I just met him. I don't know who he is, but I do feel compassion for him. I feel sorry that he is unable to hear. I honestly wish Paul could hear. Please, Father, come fill me up with You. Fill me up with Your love and touch him. I know that after I pray, he probably won't be healed, so Father, I just pray that he won't feel rejected or unworthy. I pray that after I pray for him, he will feel loved and accepted by You, Father.*

All during this prayer I did not move my lips. I just thought this prayer to the Father. Then I looked at Paul, who was standing there with a big smile, and I asked if I could touch his ears.

When he nodded, I gently touched his ears and prayed out loud, "Father, shower Paul with Your love. Let him know You more. Let him feel Your love for him. Touch him, Lord. Fill him with Your unconditional love." Then I began to pray as the Spirit led me: "I break any rejection in your life, Paul. I break any curses, even those released over you in the womb."

I had prayed a short prayer, not longer than a minute. When I finished, Paul had tears in his eyes.

I smiled at him and said, "Can I give you a hug?"

He nodded, his face filled with tears.

I gave him a big bear hug and said, "Father God loves you, Paul. Father God loves you."

"I know . . ." he answered. "I know He loves me."

I jerked myself away from him, saying, "Wait a minute . . . how could you answer me if you couldn't see my lips when I said it?"

"I heard you." He laughed.

"What?" I asked in disbelief.

"I can hear you," he said.

Rob, who had been interceding next to us all along, started screaming and jumping up and down with joy.

"Wait a minute," I said again, not quite sure what was happening. "You mean you can hear me, really?"

"Yes," Paul answered, "I can hear you. I can hear every thing!" He started pointing at things around us. "I can hear that car passing by! I can hear that bird singing! I can hear that guy's cell phone ringing! I can hear people singing inside the church!"

"Wait a minute, Rob. Is this a joke? Did you set me up?"

You can tell how much faith I had for that healing to take place. My faith had nothing to do with Paul's healing—that much I know for sure.

"This is the real deal, bro," Rob said, slapping me on my shoulder.

I was not convinced. "Paul . . . were you really deaf?"

"Yes, Ed, I was totally deaf from birth."

"And now," I stuttered, "what percentage can you hear?"

"One hundred percent," he said with a smile.

"Okay, stay here and don't turn around. I'm going to stand behind you and say a few words. I want you to repeat them after me," I instructed. "I'll say a word, and if you get it right, I'll take a step away. I want to see how far away you can hear me."

"Yes, no problem," Paul answered excitedly.

I stood behind him and said the first word: "Jesus."

Sure enough, Paul repeated, "Jesus."

I took a couple of steps back and said, "Glory."

Paul repeated, "Glory."

By now Rob was doing cartwheels, literally.

"Hallelujah," I said, now about ten feet away from Paul.

"Hallelujah," he repeated.

I continued for another three words, but then, being the great man of faith that I am, I thought: *I'm saying all these Christian words, and maybe he's just guessing them. I'm going to try something different.*

"Banana," I said.

Paul turned around with a big smile, pointed at me, winked and said, "Banana!"

Rob shouted, "Praise Jesus!" and the three of us hugged and cried, thankful to the Father that He would answer our prayers and heal the sick.

I went back with Randy to that city one year later. When I got there, Paul brought his wife, Claudia, who was also deaf from birth. On that night God sovereignly healed over twenty-five people in the deaf section, nearly emptying it. Claudia, Paul's wife, was in that section and was totally healed.

Here is a key principle in the healing ministry: Whenever you pray, be it for healing, deliverance or even for the dead to be raised, love must be your motivation. Love is what motivated Jesus during His ministry on the earth. In fact, being motivated by love will bring you success in any area of your life. Have compassion for others and surrender to God. When your heart is filled with love and compassion for others, when you submit to God every step of the way, then the Father will perform great works through your life.

Ears to Hear

Since that day, 112 deaf ears have been healed when I have prayed. Keep in mind that this number represents more people than you might first realize. I count the number of individual ears healed since some people were deaf only in one ear, while others were deaf in both ears. I remember many of these people's faces and stories, as well as their joy and tears. I remember the lady in British Columbia who had lost her hearing at a young age because a soldier had punched her continuously on the side of her head. She was totally deaf in the left ear, and Jesus healed her.

I remember the teenage young lady in Florida who was deaf in her right ear. Her mother had lost her faith, but that night she went with her insistent daughter to the service. This mother could not hold back her tears and she dedicated her life again to Christ as she witnessed her daughter receive total healing.

I remember the young man in Brazil who had lost all hearing in his left ear because of a diving accident. As I prayed for him, I asked him to snap his fingers close to his left ear. As he snapped his fingers, this translucent liquid, much like water, ran down from his left ear and he started to hear again. He had been deaf in that ear for ten years, and today he is totally healed.

Recently, I had the joy of praying for one more deaf young man in Brazil. His name is Rafael, and he was deaf in his left ear from birth.

In front of the entire congregation, I laid my hands on his ears and told the church, "Watch this! If you have your cell phones pull them out and record this, because Jesus is about to open this young man's deaf ear!"

With a simple prayer, Rafael's ear opened. For the first time in his life, he could hear out of that ear.

God is so good, and I am thankful that He has given us, His children, the honor of being used by Him to bring healing to the sick. All things are possible with God. Ever since that first deaf boy I prayed for, I have learned so much from Him. As I continue to press deeper into the mysteries of the healing ministry, I have made a decision to remember that love is the driving force behind the miracle. I want to encourage you to let love lead you. Let love motivate you in all you do. Be filled with God's love.

Todd White, my friend and a powerful evangelist, once told me this about healing: "Bro, it's not about having another testimony to tell in church. It is about really caring for that one person's need."

He is absolutely right. It is all about love, because God is love, and without God, without love, we can do nothing!

Prayer for Healing

I know I have been telling you about how I learned to pray for others and how you can do the same, but now I want to stop for a moment and pray for you. If you need healing for your ears, I believe it is God's will for you to be healed, and I want to pray with you. As I have shared here, the Father has given me a special grace for healing deaf ears. Words cannot express how much faith I have for your ears to be opened. I have so much faith for healing of deaf ears that I believe that the Holy Spirit may have already started to heal you right now! I want to pray this prayer with you. Lay hands on your deaf ear(s) and repeat this prayer out loud:

Dear heavenly Father, thank You for Your love for me. Thank You for sending my Jesus to die on the cross for me. Thank You that His body was bruised for my healing as much as His blood was shed for my salvation. Thank You that Jesus took my infirmities upon Himself on the cross.

Now, in the name and authority of Jesus, I command this ear to open. If a spirit of infirmity causes this deafness,

I take authority over it now. I command it to leave this minute and never come back! I command all deafness to leave now in Jesus' name.

Come, Holy Spirit. Fill me up, touch me and bless me in Jesus' mighty name. Amen!

Now check your ears. Snap your fingers next to the deaf ear(s) and see if there is any improvement. It is very important to be thankful for the little things. If there was any increase in your hearing at all, even if it was minor, I want you to express your gratitude to the Father by praising Jesus and thanking Him for what He has done.

When you feel as though you have experienced a considerable amount of healing—for example, let's say you think you have reached 80 percent healing or more—I want you to clap your hands ten times and thank Jesus for your miracle. You do not have to wait until you are 100 percent healed before you give glory to God for working a miracle in you. In fact, if people reach a considerable amount of healing, even though it is not yet 100 percent, and they do not give glory to God, doubt can kick in and they can lose their healing. But if they feel they are mostly healed and they start to testify, it consolidates their healing in their hearts and minds and they often go on to reach 100 percent. So if you were healed a considerable amount with this prayer, I want to know about it. Please send your testimony to info@edrocha.org. I would be delighted to hear about what the Lord has done for you.

2

The Blind See

Faith versus Fear

Jesus said to him, "Receive your sight; your faith has healed you." Immediately he received his sight and followed Jesus, praising God.

Luke 18:42–43

The full moon was shining high in the dark blue sky, as the smell of sweet popcorn from the vendors outside wafted into the gymnasium. The place was packed with twenty thousand Spirit-filled and revival-hungry Brazilians. The meeting started out incredibly and only got better as the night went on. We started praying for the sick toward the end of the night, and many deaf ears were opened. Many people walked out of wheelchairs. Many stroke victims were healed of their partial paralysis. The worship team praised the Lord with a choir of thousands of voices, all passionately exalting the name of Jesus. It was heaven on earth.

As I stood there praying for the sick with the team in front of the stage, I saw people with all sorts of illnesses being healed. Suddenly, a man walked up to me with black shades on, holding a cane. I knew he was blind, and up to that point I had never prayed for a blind person. I had seen others pray for them and had seen dozens of blind people healed, but I had never personally laid hands on a blind eye and prayed for the Lord to restore it. As soon as I saw this man approach, my heart raced and my mouth went dry.

I had always considered myself a bold person. I had no idea that this fear was there, stalking inside, waiting for the right time to manifest. I realized at that moment that I had been avoiding having to pray for people with blind eyes. I had seen some pretty bad cases being healed when I prayed, even leprosy and cancer. I had laid hands on people in wheelchairs and seen them get up and walk, but I had never prayed for the blind.

"Hold My Cane"

Our Father in heaven is such a great Papa. He knew I would be standing there that night with that blind man in front of me. He also knew I would not have been ready for it on my own, so He had trained me. Just a few months prior to that meeting, I had been preaching with my spiritual brother Marcelo Casagrande. Marcelo is another Brazilian spiritual son of Randy Clark, and he is well advanced in the healing ministry.

I had been invited to do a three-night healing school at a large church in São Paulo, and I had invited Marcelo to come with me. We were having a great time doing the healing school. Father God was showing up in every meeting, and hundreds of people were being healed every night. On the last night I preached on faith, one of my favorite subjects. I preached on Mark 9:23, that all things are possible for those who believe.

At the end of the message I did an activation prayer and told the people to lay hands on each other and pray for healing.

Right beside Marcelo that night was a blind lady named Julia. She had been blind for more than a decade. She wore black sunglasses inside the church so that her severely deformed eyes would not distract other people. When I told the church to lay hands on others next to them, Marcelo jumped right at her.

At that point, Marcelo had already healed—or rather, God had healed through Marcelo—twelve blind eyes. He had so much faith for the healing of the blind that when I released the church to pray, he jumped right to Julia's side, introduced himself and asked if he could pray for her. Before he prayed, he started to tell her testimonies about the blind that he had witnessed being healed since Randy had prayed for him to receive an impartation of healing anointing six years prior to that moment. After sharing a few testimonies, he quoted some healing Scriptures to her.

Marcelo was demonstrating two of the most important principles in the healing ministry: the power of the testimony and the power of the Word of God. John describes the power of this foundation, testifying to "the word of God and the testimony of Jesus Christ" (Revelation 1:2). These are two key elements necessary to build the amount of faith a supernatural healing requires. (A third key element is worship, and I will talk about that one in more detail in chapter 6.) After praying for and seeing thousands of people healed in the ten years I have been involved in the healing ministry, I have noticed that many more people are healed when they hear a teaching about healing using these two key elements:

1. Scripture: Quote the Word of God to people, specifically passages related to healing, such as Isaiah 53:4–5, Matthew 8:16 and Luke 9:11.

2. Testimony: Share testimonies of healings with people, especially healings related to whatever problem they may have.

There is power in the Word of God, and there is power in the testimony of Jesus. When these two factors combine, it unlocks something in the spiritual realm that releases power to heal the sick. The Word of God points to the promise. The testimony of Jesus points to the fulfillment of the promise. When you combine both, they act like dynamite and fire. Dynamite has the potential to explode, but it will not do anything unless you fire it up. So it is with the *logos*, the Word, too. God's Word has the potential to heal, but it needs to be fired up by the testimony of Jesus. When people hear the proclamation of the Word, the promises of God, it creates hope in them. Once they have hope, if they hear the testimony of Jesus, who is the incarnation and fulfillment of God's promises, their hope turns into faith. Where there is faith, miracles take place: "Continue securely established and steadfast in the faith, without shifting from the hope promised by the gospel that you heard" (Colossians 1:23 NRSV).

Julia had heard the proclamation of the promises in the Word of God and had just finished hearing some wonderful healing testimonies about people who had the same issue as she had. She was ready for her miracle.

"Can I take my shades off?" she asked Marcelo with a big smile on her face. Her joy was obvious. The dynamite was ready to explode.

Marcelo looked at me and laughed because he had seen this before, and he knew what was about to happen. He called me, and I came down off the stage. The Holy Spirit had taken over the service anyway, so I was not preaching anymore. I released people to lay hands on the sick in the congregation, and they were clapping and cheering as they saw God heal people through the simple yet powerful prayer, "Come, Holy Spirit."

Marcelo laid hands on Julia's deformed eyes and repeated the same simple prayer. When he took off his hands, she had brand-new eyes.

"Hold my cane," she said, folding up her white cane and handing it to her friend beside her.

"Are you better?" Marcelo asked. "What can you see?"

Julia did not say a word. She could not speak because she was in total shock. She walked around the church to look at the colors, the paintings, the flags, the people and all that she had not been able to see in the last several years since she had lost her vision. The pastor's wife came running toward her and embraced her with a hug, but Julia pushed her away.

"Julia, it's me, your pastor," the pastor's wife said to her.

"Oh, sorry!" Julia said, laughing. "Now that I hear you speak I recognize your voice, but at first I thought, *Who is this crazy woman grabbing me like this?*" Julia had been a church member for five years and had never seen her pastor's face.

We took Julia up on the stage to share her testimony. For years she had been blind, and now she could see. The church went crazy, South American style—clapping, cheering and shouting the name of Jesus with passion. Many people got healed after they saw what God had done for Julia. At the end we did an altar call, and hundreds of visitors gave their lives to Jesus, amazed at the revelation that indeed He is the same yesterday, today and forever. It reminded me of what happened in Mark 3:8–10:

> When they heard about all he was doing, many people came to him from Judea, Jerusalem, Idumea, and the regions across the Jordan and around Tyre and Sidon. . . . For he had healed many, so that those with diseases were pushing forward to touch him.

When I saw that Marcelo did not dodge the blind woman, but actually jumped at her, asking eagerly to pray for her, a light

38

switch went on in my head. *He sees blindness as an opportunity to glorify God*, I thought. *It's all a matter of perspective.*

"I See Everything"

Up to that point I had seen blindness as an opportunity for me to feel embarrassed if nothing happened. That mindset had led me to avoid praying for the blind. When I saw the joy in Marcelo's face as he spoke to that lady, however, I understood that he saw her blindness as an opportunity to bring glory to the name of Jesus. For the first time, I finally understood what Jesus meant in this passage of Scripture:

> As he passed by, he saw a man blind from birth. And his disciples asked him, "Rabbi, who sinned, this man or his parents, that he was born blind?" Jesus answered, "It was not that this man sinned, or his parents, but that the works of God might be displayed in him."
>
> John 9:1–3 ESV

A few months had passed since that healing with Marcelo, and there I was at the gymnasium, standing in front of the blind man whom the Father had sent my way. After having seen with my own eyes what God can do through a man like Marcelo whose heart is completely His, I asked with a smile, "What would you like me to pray for you?"

I know this sounds like a silly question to ask a blind man who wants prayer, but it is not. Sometimes we forget that the blind may also have other conditions—anything a sighted person might have, from migraines to kidney stones to back problems to arthritis to carpal tunnel. In our ministry we have prayed for thousands of blind and deaf people who came forward for prayer about several other conditions. When I ask what someone wants prayer for, there is also a principle in operation: I cannot do for you what you do not believe for. So I ask people what kind of healing they are seeking, because it is about the power of agreement. Jesus said, "Again, truly I tell you that if two of you on earth agree about anything they ask for, it will be done for them by my Father in heaven" (Matthew 18:19). This is why Jesus would ask people what they wanted Him to do for them, so that He could come into agreement with them.

"I want to see," this blind man told me. Black sunglasses covered his eyes, and he held his foldable white cane in his right hand.

It was at that moment that fear struck—cold, sharp and deep within me. But I asked him, "What's your name?"

"Nicolas."

"Okay, Nicolas. What percentage of your sight have you lost?"

"All of it. I lost all my sight in both eyes." He lowered his head and continued, "I can't see at all."

"And how long have you been blind?"

"It came on gradually. I lost my eyesight little by little because it's a degenerative condition. The last time that I remember seeing anything, I was ten."

"How old are you now?"

"Thirty-three."

"So you've been blind for over twenty years?"

"Yes."

I took a deep breath. My palms were sweaty, but this time I knew what to do. I started quoting every Scripture I could remember about God's love. After having Nicolas repeat the Scriptures after me, I shared the testimony of what Jesus had done to Julia in São Paulo. The interesting thing is that by this point, I did not have one ounce of fear left in me. As I started to quote Scriptures about God's love, all the fear left. Do you know why? Because as this man and I proclaimed God's Word, our hearts and minds were filled with the promise of His perfect love: "There is no fear in love, but perfect love casts out fear" (1 John 4:18 ESV).

I could tell Nicolas's faith had grown, too, so when the time came for us to pray, I told him to take off his sunglasses. He had had those shades on for so long that now, without them, he looked like a raccoon. The skin of his face was tan, but the skin around his eyes was pale.

"Close your eyes," I instructed. I started to pray the simple prayer that never fails: "Come, Holy Spirit." I waited on the Lord for a minute or two, repeating this simple prayer that I had learned from Randy, and then I took my hands off and said, "Look around, Nicolas. Tell me if there has been any improvement."

He did not say a thing. He started looking around, and then he folded up his white cane and gave it to his wife, who was standing behind him. For the first time in many years, Nicolas walked around, not cautiously like a blind man, but freely and securely, with firm steps.

"Tell me what you see," I said with excitement.

"I see everything! I see that man with the checkered shirt. I see that lady with the blue dress . . ." And on he went, walking around and describing the colors and shapes of the world he could see, a world that for so long had been behind a veil of darkness, but was now made clear by the light of Christ.

I was in shock. It was so simple, yet all these years I had been, much like Nicolas, blind to the truth of the world of possibilities around me. *It's all about how I see it*, I thought.

The Most Important Factor

The first and most important factor in healing is *faith*. Without faith we cannot have a relationship with God, and we are doomed to a sad life on earth and eternity in hell. What is faith? Faith is a revealed assurance that something is true; it is the "I know that I know" mentality.

The Bible says that faith is "the assurance of things hoped for, the conviction of things not seen" (Hebrews 11:1 ESV). Once we receive this assurance from God, our part is then to respond to that revelation with actions that align with what we say we believe.

If we fail to establish an atmosphere of faith, we rely only on a natural mentality, a religious mindset. A natural and religious environment is rocky, unplowed soil where the seeds of miracles wither and die. A religious mindset holds people hostage in a powerless Christianity that prevents them from getting and keeping their healing.

Christianity without power is like a shiny red car without an engine. It may look good on the outside, but it will not take you anywhere. Let's pop the hood and put an engine in that thing! Let's have some miracles take place in our lives and in the lives of others around us. And for miracles to take place, we need faith. Without faith it is impossible to please God, and without an atmosphere of faith, we cannot experience the fullness of the Kingdom (see Hebrews 11:6). We must pave our way with faith before we can see miracles happen.

When the Penny Dropped

One night at a different meeting, the presence of God fell on us. Bodies were everywhere. People were being baptized in the Holy Spirit; some were laughing, some were crying, and some were laughing and crying. Some were lying on the ground in the fetal position as God healed them of deep emotional wounds. Many came to the front for healing. This young man approached me, asking if I would pray for him.

"Sure," I said. "What can I pray for you?"

"I can't see out of my right eye," he said, pointing to his eye.

"What percentage of your vision have you lost?" I asked.

"About 85 percent."

"Okay," I said, "let's pray."

As I raised my hand to touch his blind eye, the Father spoke to me and said, *Where does the power to heal come from?* I heard it as clear as day inside my heart.

From You, Father, I answered.

Do you feel My power to heal here now? He asked me.

Yes, Father, I do.

Then why do you pray long prayers?

I was new to healing the blind, so because of my insecurity and lack of wisdom about how such a miracle takes place, I would pray long prayers in order to "give it time," thinking it would take time for the miracle to manifest. Even without full understanding on my part, by God's grace people were still being healed. With time and experience, however, I came to learn that just because something is working does not mean it is working in the best way possible. With the right equipment, we can get done in one hour what would otherwise take us the whole day to finish. In the same way, we must always ask God to bring us new and fresh revelation for the work of the ministry. He can give us the best way to get more done with less effort.

This is especially true concerning the healing ministry, which is surrounded by misconceptions, controversy and mystery. When God asked me why I was praying long prayers, the penny dropped.

Because I'm insecure, I answered.

Why are you insecure? Are you the one with power to heal?

God's voice sounded reassuring, like that of a kind and loving Teacher.

No, Father, You are. I'm sorry. I get it. The power to heal comes from You, and it is present here right now. I'll pray a quick prayer.

How quick? asked the Father.

One minute? I asked, unsure.

How about one second?

I smiled, feeling confidence rising within me. This internal conversation happened in only a few seconds. The man had his eyes closed, and I placed the tips of my index and middle fingers on his blind eye and prayed, "Thank You, Jesus!" As I did, in the spirit I saw a bluish electric wave of power flow from me into his eye.

Ask him to check it out, the Father told me.

"Open your eyes. Cover the one that was good and check to see how the one that was blind is now," I told him.

He covered the eye that was good and looked around with the eye that had been blind. As he did, he started to laugh.

"Is it better?" I asked, smiling.

"Yes, yes!" he said, laughing.

"How much better?"

"It's all the way. I can see normally with this eye now." He closed the right eye and opened the left, looked around and then switched back and forth from his left to his right eye. "Actually"—he laughed again, showing his large, white teeth—"I can see better now with the healed eye."

"One . . . Two . . . Five"

I was recently with Randy in the south of Brazil. God was using him to heal many sick people, especially the terminally ill. Lately Randy has shown a great interest in praying for the worst cases—those with cerebral palsy, cancer, paralysis, strokes and other terminal illnesses. God is giving him great favor to heal them. As he was praying for a line of terminally ill people, a lady with a blind eye came to him and asked him to pray. Sharply dressed, she was clearly from the middle class. Her blind eye looked as normal as her other eye. Had she not told us she was blind in that eye, we would never have guessed.

Pointing to me, Randy turned to her and said, "Ed will pray for you. I want to focus on the terminally ill."

I quickly got another translator to take over for me and went to pray for her. "Which eye is the blind one? I can't tell," I said.

She smiled at me and pointed to her right eye.

"What's wrong with it? It looks perfectly normal to me."

"I was born totally blind in this eye," she said. "I've been to many specialists, and they all say there's nothing wrong with my eye and that they don't understand why it doesn't work."

"Well, if the hardware is fine, then maybe there's a problem with the software," I concluded. I had no idea where that affirmation came from. I just heard the words come out of my mouth.

As I put my hands on her, I prayed, "Father, according to the doctors all the hardware in this lady's eye is just fine." I raised my other hand. "In the name of Jesus I command all the software that she needs for this eye to work to be written in her brain now. I command all the neural connections to be made, and that this software will be downloaded, synced and updated from the cloud from heaven."

I lowered my hands. "Check it out now. Cover the eye that was already good and look around with the other one. Is it better?"

"Yes!" she said, smiling. "It's all blurry, but I can see now. I see color."

"What did you see out of it before?"

"Nothing. If I closed my left eye, I would see as much as you do with both eyes closed," she explained.

"And how is it now?"

"Now I can see. It's blurry, but I can see."

"Okay, praise Jesus," I said. "Just give it a few seconds for your brain to adapt to the new software from heaven."

"It's improving!" she said, looking around. Covering her left eye with her hand and now seeing out of the eye that was blind, she said, "I can see clearly now."

"Tell me how many fingers I'm showing you."

"One . . . two . . . five," she said as I stood about ten feet away from her. She was right each time.

"And you could not see this before?" I asked, trying to provoke a reaction because she was having a classic "in shock" response to her healing. She was not showing any exterior signs of joy or happiness, and I could tell that her mind was having a hard time trying to wrap around the fact that she could now see out of that formerly blind eye. I wanted to help her realize that she was healed; I wanted to help her mind accept the fact that this was her new reality. So I asked questions that made her compare her previous state to her current state of healing, so that her emotions would kick in: happiness, tears of joy, laughter and all the good signs of gratitude that should follow a healing, especially a major healing like this.

"No," she told me, "I could not see out of this eye at all, and now I can."

The people around us started to clap and praise the name of Jesus.

"Wherever you go, tell people about what Jesus has done for you," I told her.

"I will," she answered, tears of joy and gratitude now falling from her face. "I certainly will."

Prayer for Healing

Since the first blind eye I prayed for, I have now prayed for eight blind eyes that have been opened. My faith for blind eyes to open increases with every blind person I pray for. The Father wants you to have perfect vision, and you should believe and press in for your healing. If you need healing for your eyes, I want you to pray the following prayer with me. Take off any glasses or lenses you may have on, gently lay your hands over your eyes and say this prayer out loud:

> *Heavenly Father, thank You for Your love. Thank You for accepting me as Your child. Thank You that healing is the bread of the children.*
>
> *In the name and authority of Jesus, I command my eyes to be healed! I command all the cells in my eyes to be restored. I command all that is wrong with my eyes to be fixed now! In Jesus' name, let it be on earth as it is in heaven. In the name and authority of Jesus, I bless my eyes with perfect vision. Thank You, Jesus!*

If you prayed this prayer and your vision was healed a considerable amount (remember, in chapter 1 I explained that as 80 percent or more), I want to hear about it. In fact, whatever illness you have, if you are healed at any point as you read this book, I want you to let me know so that I can rejoice and celebrate your healing with you. As I said at the end of the first chapter, you can send me an email with your testimony. (My contact information is at the end of the book.)

If you did not experience a considerable healing in your vision yet, don't give up. Press in. You may have to pray this prayer more than once. Remember that even Jesus had to pray for a certain blind man twice before he was totally healed (see Mark 8:22–25). I want to encourage you to believe and press in for your healing. It is God's will for you to have perfect vision. Have faith and keep praying. Your healing will come!

3

The Lame Walk

Hear and Obey

"Stand up, take your bed and go to your home." And he stood up and went to his home.

Matthew 9:6–7 NRSV

Years before I heard about the Toronto Blessing, I was translating for a guest speaker from North America at a Revived Methodist church during a worship conference. On the last night, as the whole church sang passionately to the Lord and celebrated His love, a man came rolling down the aisle toward the stage in his wheelchair. I don't know how he came up with the idea that he could be healed that night. Nobody was talking about healing. Nobody mentioned that we would pray for the sick; none of the leaders were even planning on it. In fact, the speaker was a worship leader with zero experience in praying for the sick.

The whole church was standing and worshiping. Now remember, this is Brazil. If you have never been in a worship service in Brazil, you don't know what you are missing. Down here, we take praising the Lord seriously. We worship with passion, which includes a lot of moving, dancing and sweating. There were hundreds of young men and women up front jumping and praising God, and from the midst of them came that man, slowly yet surely making his way to the front.

When I saw that wheelchair coming, I looked into the man's eyes and saw that he had faith to be healed. For the first time I totally understood Mark 11:24, "Whatever you ask for in prayer, believe that you have received it, and it will be yours." I knew that this man had that heart.

The stage was only three feet high, so the man in the wheelchair grabbed the edge of my pant leg and pulled it as if he were ringing a church bell. It was a good thing I had a belt on that night! I bent down and looked at him inquisitively.

"Yes, sir?" I asked, shouting at him over the loud music and stomping all around us.

"Pray for me!" he shouted back.

Up to that point I had never prayed for a lame person to walk. I had never seen anyone else do it, either. That was the sort of thing I only read about in the Bible.

"Pray for me," he said again. "I want to walk." His eyes were filled with conviction and faith.

"Okay," I said, "let me get the preacher to pray for you."

As I turned around, the man grabbed me and said firmly, "No, you're the one. I want you to pray for me."

"But I'm only the translator," I replied with a smile. Though I had been a preacher for many years by this point, I still wanted to honor the speaker since I was there to act as his translator. And more importantly, this gave me a great excuse to avoid praying for the man since I had no idea what to do. I reached out to the speaker, who, like everybody else, had seen the lame man coming toward us in the wheelchair. The speaker had turned his back to me and had his hands lifted in worship, though I saw him peek at me a couple of times from the corner of his eye. I came near him and touched his shoulder, and he leaned his head close to mine.

"This man wants to be prayed for," I shouted near his ear. "He believes he can walk again."

"Good. You pray for him," he said and turned away, raising his hands in worship.

"But you're the speaker. I'm only the translator."

He placed a hand over his mouth so I could hear him better and said, "I feel this one is for you. Go ahead and pray for him."

I did not know what to do, but I knew that I was not going to send the lame man away. I could tell by looking into his eyes that he was determined to receive healing that night. I jumped down from the stage and told him I was going to pray for him.

"I knew you were supposed to pray for me. If you pray for me, I will walk," he affirmed.

Looking back, I know it was the Lord who put this determination in the man to be healed because of my prayer. But at the time, I had no idea what was happening or how the man had come to that conclusion.

"What's your name?" I asked.

"Carlos."

"Carlos," I began, "how long have you been in this wheelchair?"

"I had a car accident six years ago, and I haven't walked since."

"Can you move your feet?"

"No. I can't feel anything below my waist."

I stood beside his wheelchair and put my hands on his shoulders. I closed my eyes and prayed silently under my breath, *Dear God, have mercy on me. I have no idea what I'm doing. Have mercy on this man, too. He has so much faith that he*

will walk. I, on the other hand, am not so sure of that myself.
Have mercy on me for his sake. I don't want to be the reason
he doesn't get healed. So please, heal my unbelief.

Obviously, my style of prayer and my level of faith were not
going to be the reasons a miracle took place.

Tell him to walk, and he will walk, I heard the Father say
within my spirit.

What? I asked. *How does that work?*

No answer.

I had been a Christian all my life and a pastor for many years,
but there was still much that needed to be done in my heart,
mind and spirit in terms of having a true, deep relationship
with God. My level of intimacy with Him was very small, and
I was still very religious. Most of the time when I prayed, He
would not answer back, or at least that was the impression I
had. Maybe He was answering and I just did not have ears to
hear, as it says in Scripture. Either way, I thought that was the
norm for everyone.

Listening to God's voice was a rarity for me, so when I heard
Him say, *Tell him to walk, and he will walk,* I did not understand it. But I went with it because that was all I had. I knew
one thing only: It was definitely God who had spoken. I might
not have known much about the healing ministry at the time,
but one thing I had learned in all those years of living in total
dependence on God as a missionary was how to distinguish
His voice. In the rare times I did hear Him, I knew whose voice
it was.

With the assurance in my heart that it was God speaking to
me, I told the paralyzed man, "God just told me to tell you,
Walk, and you will walk."

I paused, and we stared at one another. "Does that make
any sense to you?" I wrinkled my face as if I had just sucked
on a lemon.

"Yes," he said, pausing, "it does."

As he said that, he grabbed on to my arm as though his life depended on it and tried to pull himself up. I gave a head signal to one of the young men around us to help him. As the young helper started to grab Carlos's arm, I instructed him not to pull him up, but to bend down and make it easier for Carlos to place his arm around him. Now, I know that the Spirit was leading me, but when it was going on, I had no clue where that idea had come from. Carlos put his arms around me and the other young man and pulled himself up. His legs, which had not been used for six years, wriggled involuntarily, like wet noodles. He tried to stand on them, but they would not respond.

"Walk, and you will walk," I reminded him.

He nodded at me, and then, with a swing of his hip, he threw his right leg in what looked almost like a step. Both the young helper and I took a step forward. Carlos threw his left hip forward, and his noodle-like leg followed. People all around us started to open a gap in the crowd of worshipers for us to pass through. For the first three steps nothing really happened; we just carried a crippled man on our shoulders. After the third step, however, something supernatural happened. For the first time in six years, Carlos's leg started to move again.

Carlos laughed and stared at me with a wide smile. Then his other leg started to move. Now he was not throwing his hips anymore. He was actually moving his legs and forming steps. Because his legs had not been used in six years and his muscles had atrophied, there was still no way that they would be able to hold his weight. From the waist up Carlos was a strong man in his thirties, but from his waist down he looked like a skinny teenager with chopsticks for legs. We figured that just being able to move his legs at all was already a great improvement since they were basically noodles to start with.

The crowd started to cheer as we walked around the church building with him on our shoulders. As we completed the loop and got to the starting point in front of the altar, I told my young helper to let go, and he came out from under him. Carlos looked at his legs and then at me with an uncontrollable and beautiful smile.

"I'm walking!" he exclaimed.

"Yes, you are!" I said back.

I smiled at him with the cool assurance of someone who saw this kind of thing every day right after breakfast. What had changed in me? How did I go from praying for my faith to be healed to fully believing Carlos would walk that night? At some point after I had decided to act on the word God gave me, the warm blanket of the anointing fell upon me. I knew I was not alone in this, and I had no more questions, only answers; no more doubts, only certainties. I knew the man would be totally healed.

We went around one more lap, and at this point everyone in the church was staring at this amazing miracle. After we completed the second lap I let go of him, and he walked by himself. The crowd went wild, cheering and laughing and clapping, while some covered their mouths and cried.

Our young helper knelt on the ground and started to pull chunks of hair out of his head, screaming: "He's for real! He's for real! Jesus is God!"

Intense excitement at seeing the miraculous is understandable, but having someone pull out chunks of hair seemed like a shocking reaction. I knew that young helper personally, however, and I knew he was not living a life of holiness and consecration. Much to the contrary! He was a lukewarm Christian, and in this moment I think he was struck with the sudden realization that all he had heard about Jesus was really true. I believe that when he came to that realization and contrasted it with his sinful lifestyle, it caused a great feeling of repentance to come on him, which he expressed by pulling out his hair. Perhaps his reaction was similar to that of the sinner who punched himself in the chest in one of Jesus' parables: "But the tax collector stood at a distance and dared not even lift his eyes to heaven as he prayed. Instead, he beat his chest in sorrow, saying, 'O God, be merciful to me, for I am a sinner'" (Luke 18:13 NLT).

I saw a woman following Carlos a few steps behind us, crying.

"Are you a relative?" I asked her.

"Yes, I'm his wife," she said, "and I haven't seen him do this in six years."

After the third lap Carlos stopped in front of the altar and said he was tired. His skinny, teenage-like legs were trembling underneath him. Someone quickly brought him his wheelchair.

"No!" Carlos pointed at the wheelchair sternly, with the determination of a warrior who had just fought for his life. "I will never sit in that thing again."

I pulled a regular chair behind him, and he sat on it, smiling and telling me how grateful he was to me.

"I didn't have anything to do with this, Carlos," I told him. "This healing is yours and God's. You were the one who believed from the start."

"Yes, but you heard and obeyed," he said with light in his eyes, "and for that I'm eternally grateful."

Carlos left the church building with his wife by his side, walking on his own legs. It reminded me of one of the miracles we read about in the book of Acts:

> In Lystra there sat a man who was lame. He had been that way from birth and had never walked. He listened to Paul as he was speaking. Paul looked directly at him, saw that he had faith to be healed and called out, "Stand up on your feet!" At that, the man jumped up and began to walk.
>
> Acts 14:8–10

Since that day, in my almost ten years now ministering with Randy Clark, I have seen dozens of people walk out of wheelchairs. Randy once prayed for a man with multiple sclerosis who had not been able to move anything below his neck for over five years. I watched as this man slowly started to move again, eventually getting up from his wheelchair and walking toward his wife's outstretched arms. This is just one of the thousands of healings and miracles we have captured on video so that others can see and believe that Jesus Christ is Lord—the same yesterday, today and forever.

Prayer for Healing

If you need healing for your legs, I want you to lay hands on the area where you need your healing and pray this prayer with me:

Heavenly Father, thank You for Your love. Thank You for sending Jesus to die on the cross for me. Thank You that by His stripes I am healed!

In the name and authority of Jesus, I command my legs to be healed now. I command every muscle, cartilage, ligament, bone and all the damaged areas of my legs to be healed now. I command sickness to go now. I command strength to fill my legs now in Jesus' mighty name.

Come, Holy Spirit. Touch me, fill me and strengthen me. Let Your healing power flow to my legs now in the name of Jesus. Thank You, Jesus!

Now, try to move your legs. Try to do something you could not do before. So many times people are healed when, as an act of faith, they try to do something they could not do before. Take baby steps, though. Don't try to jump out of the wheelchair. Go slowly, little by little. Try to wiggle your toe, and then try to move your foot. Try to bend that knee, then stand up on your legs, then take a step. Now, if the power of the Holy Spirit jumps on you and you feel like dancing, go ahead and dance!

All things are possible for those who believe. I want to encourage you to believe and receive your healing in Jesus' name. (And don't forget to let me know about it.) Amen!

4

The Lepers Are Cleansed

Words of Command

Jesus reached out his hand and touched the man. "I am willing," he said. "Be clean!" And immediately the leprosy left him.

Luke 5:13

My heart rejoices at the memories of all of the lepers I have seen cleansed throughout my years in the ministry. Our records contain hundreds of testimonies of leprosy and other skin-related conditions that were miraculously healed. Leprosy is a severe, infectious skin disease that causes damaging sores and even nerve damage. The evidence of leprosy dates back to ancient Egypt, and the Bible includes many accounts of those affected by leprosy, especially in the New Testament.

In Jewish culture, lepers were outcasts. They could not live among the general population and were often confined against their will in leper colonies. Whenever they moved into areas common to the general public, they were required to ring a bell to identify their presence because they were "unclean." It is interesting to note that when the Bible talks about leprosy, it also includes other skin-related disorders, since in those times any skin disease, rash or discharge was considered unclean (see Leviticus 13). Any skin-related condition was considered "defiling" to the people of God.

In Jewish culture, if a man even touched a leper, he would be considered unclean according to the Law (see Leviticus 13:45–46; Numbers 5:2). Yet when Jesus touched a leper, the effect went the other way—the leper was made clean. The purity in Jesus overcame the leper's uncleanness.

There are still cases of leprosy in our modern age, and Jesus is the same yesterday, today and forever. Through His disciples, He continues to cleanse lepers today and heal those with skin-related disorders.

Baby Skin

São Paulo, Brazil, is a city with 30 million inhabitants. We were holding an open revival conference at a Renewed Baptist church there that has an attendance of at least five thousand people. Many healings took place at this conference. Deaf ears and blind eyes were opened, the lame walked and people with skin conditions were healed. That particular church actually has fourteen thousand members spread throughout ten different congregations in neighboring cities, and there are dozens of pastors on staff. One of these pastors came to Randy Clark during the ministry time and asked for prayer. He showed Randy his arm, which was covered with white dust. It looked as though he had been making bread and had covered his arm in flour. When he brushed his skin with his fingertips, the dust fell from his arm.

"It's psoriasis," this pastor explained. "I take medicine to control it, but it just won't go away."

Randy prayed for him, rebuking the overproduction of cells, and then he blessed that pastor in the name of Jesus. It was a quick prayer, but I felt the anointing fall down on us and onto that man as Randy prayed in English and I translated into Portuguese. A year later we came back to the same church. When the time came to pray for the sick, that same pastor came to us and asked if we remembered him. Immediately my brain pulled his face from my database.

"Yes," I told him, "we prayed for you to be healed of psoriasis last year. How are you?"

"I'm fine," he said. "Tell Randy that after he prayed for me, I was made totally clean."

I was so excited about his testimony that I quickly translated our brief conversation to Randy.

Randy turned to the pastor and asked, "How long after I prayed did it take for your healing to manifest?"

"Three months," he answered. "It gradually got better, and in three months I had brand-new baby skin."

I have prayed for hundreds of people with skin conditions, and I have seen them healed by the power of the Holy Spirit in the name of Jesus. One time I was in the middle of preaching a sermon in a church in São Paulo when I had a word of knowledge for healing. I stopped the sermon and said, "There is someone here—I believe it's a middle-aged woman—and you have a skin condition. It's more severe in your hands, and it's itching so much right now that you've been biting your hands and fingers to try to find some relief. Where are you? Jesus is healing you right now."

This middle-aged woman sitting in the middle of the church stood up and said, "That's me! I have this rash that makes my skin swell and itch like crazy, so much so that I had to go to the bathroom to gnaw on my hands and fingers to try to make it stop." She started to cry.

"Did the gnawing stop the itching?" I asked.

"No, not at all," she said, wrinkling her face.

"Okay, put your hands up," I instructed. "In the name of Jesus and by the power of the Holy Spirit, I command this itching to go now and never come back!" Then I asked her to check her hands.

"It's all gone!" she exclaimed. She rubbed her hands against each other and then showed them to the crowd.

"What percentage gone would you say?" I asked.

"One hundred percent! The moment you said, 'Put your hands up,' the itching stopped, and when you finished praying, I looked at my hands, and the rash was gone!"

I also remember the testimonies of two young men from two different cities, both afflicted with psoriasis. The condition was worse on their elbows, their arms and especially their hands, where sores had broken out. After I gave a word of command in the name of Jesus, both men were totally healed, and their skin became completely clean in a few days.

Words of Command

After watching Randy pray for almost a decade, I have noticed that many times he does not ask the Father to heal. Many times he makes his prayer a command. He will either command the sickness to leave or the body to respond in a certain way. He will talk to the nerves, ligaments and immune or lymphatic system as if he were talking to a person, commanding them to function correctly.

This approach caught my attention toward the beginning of my time working with him. I started to wonder how Jesus and His disciples prayed for the sick, so I read all the healing records in the New Testament to verify how they did it and to see if they also used words of command rather than prayers of petition. I was shocked by my conclusion: All the healings and miracles performed by Jesus and His disciples came to pass by words of command! Not a single one of the healing reports in the New Testament records prayers of petition; they are all words of command. All my life I was told to ask God to heal, yet Jesus never asked the Father to heal one sick person.

You may think: *That was okay because Jesus is God, and in His divine authority He could command the sick to be healed. But we are not God, so we must ask for the healing.*

That sounds as if it should be true, but actually it is theologically wrong. Jesus did not perform one miracle out of His own divine power, but only by the power of the Holy Spirit (see Matthew 12:28). Jesus only did what He saw the Father doing, for He left His glory in heaven (see John 5:19; Philippians 2:7). Jesus came as a model for us, the firstborn of a generation who would carry the Holy Spirit of God within them. Therefore, imbued by the power of the Holy Spirit, we can fulfill Jesus' promise to us that "whoever believes in me will do the works I have been doing, and they will do even greater things than these" (John 14:12; see also Acts 1:8).

Jesus went to the Father and left us here on earth with the job of being "little Christs," little anointed ones. The origin of the term *Christ* in Old English was *Crīst*. Even further back, in Latin it was *Christus* and in Greek it was *Khristos*, meaning "anointed." From the word's origins, you can see that we Christians, as little Christs, are the anointed carriers of His presence and authority to heal the sick.

I examined every miracle and healing the apostles did, and not one of them came through prayers of petition. Rather, they were all done through words of command. Jesus' disciples learned from Him and went on healing the sick by releasing words of command, just as they had seen Him do.

This may sound a little strange, but the truth is that asking God to heal the sick is antibiblical. (I am glad I have that revelation today, but it saddens me that it took me so many years to learn it.) Let me explain what I mean. I prayed prayers of petition for healing all my life. Growing up a Christian in our church, I always prayed for the sick people who were unable to attend the meeting. Our whole church gathered together and asked God to heal the sick. We would pray fervently and ask Him to go and visit, touch and heal our sick church members wherever they were. But the funny thing is, if there were sick people in the service, we would ask how they were doing, but we would never pray for them—especially not with the laying on of hands, which was the primary way Jesus and His disciples healed the sick.[1]

When, due to our lack of understanding or teaching on the subject, we pray asking God to heal the sick, sometimes by His grace and mercy He does it. Nevertheless, when we study the subject of how Jesus and the disciples (later called apostles) prayed for healing, we see that their model for healing the sick was not through intercessory prayer. Rather, it was through words of command. We all understand that intercessory prayer has its place. When it comes to healing, however, using it is the exception, not the rule. Over the ages Christians have forgotten the rule (words of command) and have used mostly—or only—the exception (intercessory prayer) instead. And we have done it for so long that the exception has become the rule.

In the gospels Jesus clearly tells us that *we* are supposed to heal the sick. Notice that when He tells the disciples to heal the sick, He does not tell them, "Pray intercessory prayers to the Father in favor of the sick, and He will heal them." No! Jesus tells the disciples, "Heal the sick, raise the dead, cleanse those who have leprosy, drive out demons" (Matthew 10:8). Without getting into much detail in the Greek, it suffices for us to know that the verb tense Jesus used here is in the imperative: *heal*. The Lord is instructing us to do the healing, not to ask the Father to do it. Of course, we know that it is only by the power of the Holy Spirit that we can carry out this command (see Acts 1:8; 2:43).

Once you have asked for and received the Holy Spirit, you should not ask God to heal. By the power of the Holy Spirit who lives inside you and moves through you, *you* should heal the sick. For example, imagine this conversation between a father and son:

"Son . . ." a father says.

"Yes, Dad?" asks the boy, sitting on the couch.

"Take out the trash."

"Sure, Dad," the son replies before getting up and kneeling in front of his father.

"What is it, son?" the father asks.

"You are such a good father. I ask *you* to take out the trash for me. Please, do me this kindness and show mercy. Please, take out the trash."

In this case the father has already paid for the trash service to come and collect the trash from the garbage bin on the sidewalk. All the boy has to do now is put it outside, but he asks his father to do it. Consider that in this example, the trash represents sickness and the boy represents Christians. As Christians, we don't have to ask God to do what He already told us to do in the first place. We have to take action! The Father intends for us to heal the sick, so we have to command sickness to leave by the authority and in the powerful name of Jesus. Here is another example:

A police officer stops a stolen car on the streets. The car is packed with stolen goods. The thief at the steering wheel still has his ski mask on his face.

The cop pulls out his gun and yells, "Freeze! Hands in the air!"
The criminal puts his hands up and stays still, clearly fright-
ened. Then the officer grabs his radio and calls for backup.

"Dispatch, put me through to the chief—this is an emergency!"
"Go ahead—the chief is on the line."
"Chief?"
"Yes, how can I help you?"
"I've located the robbery suspect. He's sitting inside his
vehicle."
"Good job. What can I do for you?"
"Would you please come down here and make the arrest?"

Consider that in this example, the chief of police represents
God, the officer represents Christians and the thief represents
either the sickness or the demon causing the sickness. We are
not supposed to ask God to come down to do what He already
has empowered us to do. We have the authority Jesus gave us
to make the arrest: "Jesus called the twelve together and gave
them power and authority over all demons and to cure diseases"
(Luke 9:1 NRSV). You have been commissioned by Jesus to heal
the sick by the power of the Holy Spirit. He has called you
and provided you with all you need to manifest His Kingdom
in power. Don't call on the Father to ask Him to do it. Go out
there and get the job done!

You have probably heard and read about the power of our
words, and many well-known texts in Scripture teach us about
it.[2] One Scripture Christians often reference is Proverbs 18:21:
"The tongue has the power of life and death, and those who
love it will eat its fruit."

As Bill Johnson, senior pastor of Bethel Church in Redding,
California, always says, "Jesus is perfect theology," so there is no
greater model to follow in our lives and ministries than Jesus.
In Mark 11, Jesus came upon a fig tree that bore no fruit and
cursed it, saying, "May no one ever eat fruit from you again"

(verse 14). When the disciples passed by that same spot the next morning, they saw that the fig tree had withered and were amazed: "Rabbi, look! The fig tree you cursed has withered!" said Peter (verse 21). Jesus replied with a teaching:

> "Have faith in God," Jesus answered. "Truly I tell you, if anyone says to this mountain, 'Go, throw yourself into the sea,' and does not doubt in their heart but believes that what they say will happen, it will be done for them."
>
> Mark 11:22–23

This is clearly a word of command to the mountain: "Go, throw yourself into the sea." This is the same way Jesus prayed for the sick. When it came to the cleansing of the lepers, guess how Jesus healed them? That's right, words of command. The gospels record four accounts of Jesus healing men with leprosy, and in four out of four, He healed them with words of command. In the first three instances Jesus used the exact same words: "Be clean," and in the fourth He said, "Go, show yourselves to the priests" (Matthew 8:3; Mark 1:41; Luke 5:13; 17:14). He did not ask the Father to heal the lepers. In fact, He did not even pray. He commanded the healings to take place. (For more examples of the principle of healing by command throughout Scripture, see Appendix B and Appendix C at the end of this book.)

The Observer Effect

For us to better understand how words of command work, we must understand a principle exemplified best in what the scientific community calls the "observer effect." This is an idea that has puzzled scientists for years. According to Dr. Fred Alan Wolf, a respected physicist, writer and lecturer who earned his Ph.D. in theoretical physics at UCLA in 1963, the observer effect shows that reality as we know it is transformed by the eye of an observer.

Basically, we alter every object in the universe simply by perceiving it, by paying attention to it. Measurements in quantum mechanics have shown that the smallest particles of matter, upon observation, would stop whatever they were doing and gather around the measurement sensor. In his famous article "Awakening Your Soul," Dr. Wolf writes about the observer effect:

> This effect . . . first came as a big surprise to the early scientists who discovered it. They saw, at times much to their dismay that any time they attempted to perform an observation on an atomic or subatomic system, the tools they used to make the observation appeared to introduce uncontrollable errors into their measurements. . . . They soon realized that it wasn't the tools that made the errors in their determinations, but that they had stumbled on a very stubborn part of nature herself. . . . Each observation, regardless of the measuring tool employed, made its mark on the thing being observed in a completely irreversible and often unpredictable way. Whether they liked it or not, every observer ended up disturbing the thing he or she sought to look at.[3]

In plain and simple English, the observer effect shows that a particle will do what it normally does until you focus your attention on it, and then it will stop and turn to you. The first time I read this, I wondered why a particle would just stop. I was not praying about it or anything, but as soon as I had that thought, I heard, *It's waiting for your command.*

What? I asked. I knew it was the Lord.

The particle, He explained, *is waiting for your command.*

Right after I heard this, a Scripture came to my heart: "For the earnest expectation of the creation eagerly waits for the revealing of the sons of God" (Romans 8:19 NKJV).

Nature is waiting for our command. An atom is all over the place until you focus your attention on it, and then it stops.

The particle stops because it is waiting for your command. You are a child of God. Creation is waiting for your word of command. We can change matter all around us simply by focusing our attention on it and telling it what to do.

This concept totally changed the way I pray. Now when I pray to a deaf ear, I turn my attention to it and imagine the smallest particles at the molecular, atomic and subatomic levels, and I speak to these particles. I command them to be rearranged. I command them to move about and go to the right place in order for this deaf ear to be made whole and perfect, and they do. As I shared earlier, I have been having a tremendous rate of success with healing deaf ears, and I know that a great part of the reason is because I use words of command.

The discovery of the observer effect flabbergasted the whole scientific community because it turns reality into a big soup of possibilities. As Christians we already believe this, or at least we say we do. We know that we are children of God and that the world is our Father's creation. Every Christian knows—at least in theory—that the world is subject to God's children. In reality, however, as a Body we are far from calming storms.

All Things Are Possible

One of our church plants in Rio, Brazil, is a good example of what it looks like when we understand our authority in Christ. We started teaching this young church about the reality of the believer's identity and about how the universe is always waiting for our words of command. We are starting to see something beautiful unfold before us with these young Christians because they believe that everything is possible. They believe that changing the reality around them by stepping out in faith is their right and responsibility as God's children.

It is not uncommon in this church for people to affect the environment around them, literally. We were having a tent meeting one day, and it started pouring rain outside. The noise of the rain hitting the tent was so strong that we could barely hear anything else inside the tent.

Two of our disciples stood up, raised their hands toward the clouds and calmly said, "Enough. In the name of Jesus, enough."

Immediately, it stopped raining. As we were leaving the tent after the service, we started to laugh. All around us it was still raining, but there was a big hole in the dark rain clouds right above our tent.

The same thing started to happen with healing. I always empower and encourage our church members to pray for the sick. After the service we always ask those who need healing to raise their hands. Once they do, we tell the church members who are around them to lay hands on them and pray for healing. So far in our meetings, most of the people who ask for prayer are healed.

The effect this is having on the faith of our church members is indescribable. Many members go around the city and pray for people at the mall and at bus stops, laying hands on complete strangers and healing the sick. Why and how do they do that? They understand that they are children of God, and they understand their identity in Him. They understand their authority, and as they are given opportunities to exercise that authority, they blossom in power, affect the world around them and bring glory to the name of Jesus.

Prayers of Petition

There is a place for prayers of petition. Fervent prayer attracts the presence of God and releases His power to bring about healings and miracles. You can ask God whatever you want in prayer, as long as you are not asking Him to do what He already has commanded you to do. For example, you cannot ask Jesus to make disciples, for He has commanded us to do that: "Go and make disciples of all nations . . ." (Matthew 28:19).

If you are in another city and you cannot travel to pray for and lay hands on a specific person, then you can send your word of command to that person from a distance, as the centurion asked Jesus to do to heal his servant (see Matthew 8:8). But a prayer of petition could also be effective. For example, you could pray and ask God to send His holy angels with healing to that person, which is a totally valid request. However, when the sick person is within reach of your hand, you should pray for him or her with the laying on of your hands and by speaking words of command. Remember, you are not commanding God; you are commanding the sickness to leave, just as you would command a demon to leave.

In every other matter in life, you can ask God for anything that is impossible for you. You can pray words of petition for whatever you need, and whatever you pray for with faith, you will receive. Jesus said: "Therefore I tell you, whatever you ask for in prayer, believe that you have received it, and it will be yours" (Mark 11:24).

You may be thinking, *If I can pray for anything I need with faith and God will give it to me, then why can't I pray for healing with prayers of petition?*

The answer is simple: God told you and showed you through Jesus' ministry that the way to pray for physical healing is with the laying on of hands and words of command. You can pray and ask God about whatever is in your heart and whatever is troubling you. God is a good God and wants to bless us with good gifts. You can pray and ask God for the salvation of a loved one. You can pray and ask God for protection. You can pray and ask God for finances and blessings in every area of your life. You are free to ask Him to do whatever He has promised for you, but remember to do yourself what He commanded *you* to do.

You must also be careful not to pray desperate prayers—prayers based in some form of despair. Praying a desperate prayer is an oxymoron because when you pray, you do so with hope that God will answer your prayer. Being desperate implies that you have a lack of confidence and faith, and without faith, how can your prayers be answered? Your words are powerful weapons. Don't let fear and anguish take over your heart when you pray. Be sure to say good and gracious words to God, always praising Him for His faithful love toward you and keeping this Scripture in mind:

> Do not be anxious about anything, but in everything by prayer and supplication with thanksgiving let your requests be made known to God. And the peace of God, which surpasses all understanding, will guard your hearts and minds in Christ Jesus.
>
> Philippians 4:6–7 ESV

Praying with Authority

Recently, I was preaching about the Kingdom of God. After I shared the message, I called those who wanted prayer for healing to come to the front. It was one of those nights when the presence of God was so strong that it felt as though electricity were pulsing through the air. Nearly every person I prayed for was instantly healed.

All the healings in that service were amazing, but one testimony was my favorite. A woman had tumors the size of olives under her skin—dozens of them all over her body. She was related to the pastor, which I did not find out until the end of the meeting. I was praying for her just the way I pray for anyone else, when suddenly this authority came over me, and out of my mouth came words that were louder than usual and filled with . . . how can I best describe it? I will call it holy anger. I felt the righteousness of God stir up inside me; I felt the Holy Spirit's anger toward the works of the devil. I commanded the tumors to disappear, and immediately the tumor I was touching vanished from under my fingertips.

I smiled as I realized what had just happened, and I told this woman, "Check your body and see if you can find the tumors."

She checked her body and touched her arms and belly, and to her astonishment (and mine) all the tumors had immediately disappeared. I confess that I was astonished, because I had seen a few tumors disappear before, but never that fast! Usually when I prayed, tumors would shrink down to half their size, and then a few days later the people would come to me and show me that the tumors were gone. But with this lady, I mean, *bam!* Instantly gone!

I want to encourage you to believe for your healing and for healing others. Don't ask the Father to do what He already has given you the power and authority to do. Lay hands on the sick and command them to be healed in Jesus' name. If you are sick and need healing, go ahead and lay hands on yourself and command your sickness to go now in Jesus' name. God is good, and He wants you to be healed.

Remember, Elijah saw only a small cloud, yet he believed and prophesied that it would rain, and it did. What is a small cloud the size of a fist to a country devastated by three years of drought? To a person with faith, such a sign is as good as the miracle because it announces that the miracle is on the way. Elijah brought the cloud into existence by faith, and it soon became a big, torrential rain that put an end to the drought.

God likes to operate with signs like that. Some healings are immediate; others come in stages. If you have *any* sign of improvement, even a small one, remember to praise God for it and be thankful. The rain is coming!

Prayer for Healing

If you need any skin-related healing, lay hands on yourself right now and pray this prayer with me. It is important that you say it as though you mean it. There are moments when you can be nice and polite when you pray for healing, but there are also moments when you have to speak up with authority. You have to be sensitive to the Holy Spirit to discern one occasion from the other. When you pray for healing, believe what you are saying, and say it with authority. Repeat the prayer as many times as you feel you ought to—only say it with authority and faith, and you will receive your healing.

> *Dear heavenly Father, thank You for Your love. Thank You for Your presence. Come, increase Your holy presence even more here within me. I love You and want more of You. I also want You to have more of me. Take my life, take all I am, touch me and fill me.*
>
> *In the name and authority of Jesus, I command this skin condition [name the condition] to go away now and never come back! I command this condition to disappear completely from my skin in the name and authority of Jesus. I bless my skin to be totally restored. I command all that is wrong with my skin, all the cause and its effects (now name the symptoms, whether a rash, a tumor, flaky skin or whatever) to disappear now and forever in the mighty name and in the authority of my Lord Jesus Christ.*

5

The Dead Are Raised

Atmospheres of Faith

Jesus called in a loud voice, "Lazarus, come out!" The dead man came out, his hands and feet wrapped with strips of linen, and a cloth around his face.

John 11:43–44

I cannot wait for the day when raising the dead becomes just another regular attribute of the average Christian life. I believe raising the dead is like healing the sick: You are bringing God's will to earth and restoring a person's body to health. I have not raised the dead yet, but I try to do so at any opportunity. I don't show up at the funeral of complete strangers, but I have been able to pray for the dead on many occasions.

The closest I came to a resurrection was with a seven-year-old boy, the son of a married couple I know. He was a handsome, happy child, and I know beyond explanation that he was not supposed to die prematurely. I went with several of my disciples to his funeral, and together we laid hands on him and commanded life back into his body. We all felt his pulse go on and off. The boy had marks remaining on his face from the condition he had died of, and as we prayed, the marks began to diminish.

Suddenly, at the point when the boy's pulse was becoming stronger, a close relative arrived and came over. Crying out, this person threw her body on top of the child and started screaming, "Oh, my baby! Why? I can't take it!"

We made room for the grieving relative, and when we came back to pray for the child again, we did not feel anything anymore. The pulse never came back, and neither did his life. We had to accept that death had won this time.

When I look back, I see that I did everything wrong in his case. I made some basic mistakes that I will talk about in a minute. But to this day we continue to pray for the dead, and that is encouraging for our disciples at our church. We preach and teach it so much that they know they will raise the dead. It is just a matter of time and practice, like anything else. This is why our disciples pray for an average of four to six dead people every month. At every funeral they are invited to—and even at some they are not invited to—they will lay hands on the dead and pray for them. Why? Because they believe Jesus when He says that we will raise the dead, and they have heard testimonies of people who were raised from the dead (see Matthew 10:8). I will also share these testimonies with you because they will strengthen your faith. Then when the time comes, you will be prepared to bring glory to the name of Jesus in this way.

Alignment with God's Will

Raising the dead—or any other healing or miracle—can only be done in partnership with the Father. Jesus said this: "The

Son can do nothing by himself; he can only do what he sees his Father doing" (John 5:19). We cannot raise the dead or heal the sick by our own power. The power to do these things comes from God. We must align ourselves with the Father's will in order to raise the dead. If the person you are praying for is dead because God wants him or her dead, then you are wasting your time.

Think about this: Jesus had all power and all authority. He could raise anyone from the dead, correct? Then why didn't He raise John the Baptist from the dead? John was the last prophet of God's former covenant with His people, the last man to have the Holy Spirit solely upon and operating through him before the public manifestation of the Messiah and the later outpouring of the Spirit at Pentecost. Jesus said of John, "Among those born of women there has not risen anyone greater than John" (Matthew 11:11). Yet when John died, Jesus did nothing to change it. Take a look at His reaction when He heard about John's death:

> Now when Jesus heard this, he withdrew from there in a boat to a desolate place by himself. But when the crowds heard it, they followed him on foot from the towns. When he went ashore he saw a great crowd, and he had compassion on them and healed their sick.
>
> Matthew 14:13–14 ESV

Instead of raising John from the dead, Jesus went on with the mission the Father had given Him. Jesus could have gone to where John's body was, and—with only a hand gesture—broken open the gates of that prison and sent the Roman guards flying against the wall. Then, similar to what He did with the soldier whose ear Peter had cut off, He could have reattached John's head to his body and raised him from the dead. I know that sounds a little far-fetched, but one way or another, Jesus could have raised John from the dead.

Then why didn't He do it? The answer is simple: It was not the Father's will. John had fulfilled his mission on earth. He had prepared the way for Jesus to start His public ministry. That is why, instead of raising John from the dead, Jesus carried on with His calling and destiny. The driving force that was once upon John, the Holy Spirit, had departed from him and had come upon Jesus in the shape of a dove when John baptized Him. That was the Father's will. As Jesus modeled for us, you must be in alignment with the Father's will, especially when praying for the dead to be raised to life.

How do you know whether or not it is the Father's will for someone to be raised from the dead? How do you know if the person's mission is fulfilled here on earth, or if you are supposed to pray for his or her resurrection? The short answer is by listening to and being led by the Holy Spirit. But because so few Christians have experience in this area, let's look at the longer answer. You can raise the dead only if the Spirit of life in Christ Jesus is working through you, because He was the one who conquered death: "For the law of the Spirit of life in Christ Jesus has made me free from the law of sin and death" (Romans 8:2 NKJV; see also 1 Corinthians 15:55). You must be led by the Holy Spirit in order to know what the Father wants to do through you in these situations.

Yes, Jesus told us to raise the dead, but He did not mean that we should raise *all* the dead. Jesus Himself did not always raise all the dead. We know that His earthly father, Joseph, was not part of His adult life. Scholars believe that Joseph must have died sometime between Jesus' twelfth and thirtieth birthdays.[1] Even though Jesus must have loved His earthly father a lot, He did not raise him from the dead.

Neither did Jesus raise Simeon from the dead, nor the prophetess Anna, both of whom were aged at the time they saw Him as a newborn in the Temple (see Luke 2:25–38). And as I said, when Jesus heard about the death of John the Baptist, He did not go raise John from the dead, although He could have. Why didn't He? Because He only did what He saw the Father doing (see John 5:19, 30). How did Jesus know whom to raise from the dead? That brings us back to the short answer we began with: He was led by the Holy Spirit.

Faith Changes Everything

When you pray for resurrection, it is important that you only have people around you who have faith for raising the dead. The best thing to do if you are unsure about the atmosphere of faith around you is to tell everyone to leave. Only pray for the dead person to be raised once everyone has left. Unbelief kills the anointing. Where there is faith, miracles happen; where there is not faith, miracles don't happen. Sometimes our desire to be nice to people and not discourage them causes us to make room for unbelief. Miracles cannot and will not happen in an atmosphere of unbelief.

When the disciples asked Jesus why they could not cast out a demon from a boy, He addressed the main issue: "Because you have so little faith" (Matthew 17:20). Faith determines everything, and unbelief is to the power of God what glass is to electricity. You cannot conduct electricity over glass. That is why electricity companies use glass insulators on their electric poles. Unbelief insulates you from a miracle, so to speak. We see this clearly when Jesus visits His hometown, Nazareth: "And he did not do many miracles there because of their lack of faith" (Matthew 13:58). In order to get rid of unbelief, even Jesus told people to leave the house before He prayed for the dead:

> He did not let anyone follow him except Peter, James and John the brother of James. When they came to the home of the synagogue leader, Jesus saw a commotion, with people crying and wailing loudly. He went in and said to them, "Why all this

commotion and wailing? The child is not dead but asleep." But they laughed at him.

After he put them all out, he took the child's father and mother and the disciples who were with him, and went in where the child was.

Mark 5:37–40

The key here is faith. Jesus put the unbelievers out and only prayed to raise the girl from the dead with those who believed— Peter, James, John and the girl's parents. Everyone else was told to leave. When you pray for the dead, you must tell everyone to leave and make sure you only bring with you people of faith who will help you pray effectively for a resurrection.

This was my biggest mistake when I prayed for that little boy. I did not ask people to leave, and all that crying and mourning and unbelief around us broke the anointing. There were actually people complaining about how outrageous and disrespectful it was for us to lay hands on the dead boy. Many people told us we should be ashamed for bringing false hope to his parents.

This is why it is crucial for you to empty the room. If you are at a funeral, it is always best, of course, that you show respect by talking to the parents, spouse or closest relatives of the deceased person about the importance of emptying the room. Once you are alone with a few who believe, then you may go ahead and pray for a resurrection. Peter, who had been with Jesus when He raised Jairus's daughter, understood and practiced this truth: "Peter put them all outside, and knelt down and prayed; and turning to the body he said, 'Tabitha, arise.' And she opened her eyes, and when she saw Peter she sat up" (Acts 9:40 ESV).

Three Resurrections

Besides those who were raised from the dead and walked out of their tombs at the moment of Jesus' death and victory on the cross (see Matthew 27:52), we have a scriptural account of three resurrections Jesus performed in the gospels: the widow's son, Jairus's daughter and Lazarus. Jesus performed all three of these resurrections by words of command:

1. To the widow's son, He gave the command, "Get up!" (Luke 7:14).
2. To Jairus's daughter, He gave the command, "Little girl, get up!" (Mark 5:41 NLT).
3. To Lazarus, He gave the command: "Lazarus, come forth" (John 11:43 NKJV).

When Jesus raised these three from the dead, He had a direct word from the Father. Jesus always walked connected with the Father, and as I said earlier, He only did what He saw the Father doing. When He commanded the dead to rise, *boom!* In the case of the widow's son, Jesus healed whatever was wrong with the boy's body that had caused him to die, and his spirit came back to his body. The same was true with Jairus's daughter, and we see it with Lazarus as well. Jesus stopped in front of the tomb and commanded Lazarus to come forth from the grave. Suddenly, the man who had been dead for four days walked out of the tomb.

If you ever experience one of these wonderful moments when the Father clearly tells you to command the dead to be raised, make sure you don't flinch. Be ready to do what the Father tells you. Otherwise, you will miss an incredible and rare opportunity to cooperate with God and see a wonderful miracle.

Ana and Daniel's Story

Once, my friend Ana's grandson died in a boating accident at a family get-together at a lake. The ladies were preparing food and the men were having fun on their Jet Skis and boats, when suddenly something went terribly wrong. A boat and a Jet Ski collided, and Ana's teenage grandson died on impact. They brought the boy's dead body to the shore.

As you can imagine, there was a lot of crying and despair. This beautiful Christian family could not believe that such a tragedy had happened to them, but it was true. Young Daniel lay there motionless, his body broken and bleeding internally. Ana held the boy in her arms, crying and rocking him back and forth.

By the time the paramedics arrived, the boy had been dead in her arms for forty minutes. The paramedics checked on the boy and said there was nothing they could do. There was no pulse, and by the looks of the body, they confirmed that he had been dead for almost an hour.

Then something took over Ana. She stood in front of the boy's lifeless body, placed her hand on her hip and pointed nervously at him with her index finger, saying: "You listen here, Danny! This is Memaw speaking. You better come back to your body right now!" As she said this, she stomped her foot hard against the ground.

In a matter of seconds the boy's spirit came back to his body, and he started to cough out water. The paramedics rushed to the aid of the boy who had been dead for an hour, but who now lives to tell the story.

Michael and Elizabeth's Story

Another interesting case is what happened with Michael, a friend of mine, who was enjoying a beautiful summer day by the pool with his wife, son and young daughter. At some point the couple got distracted, drinking their lemonade and talking about good times, when they heard a scream. Their eleven-year-old son stood at the edge of the swimming pool, paralyzed at the sight of his little sister Elizabeth's lifeless body at the bottom of the pool. Michael quickly jumped in and dragged little Lizzie out of the water, but it was too late. She showed clear signs of asphyxiation. Her skin was covered with many purple spots, particularly on her face.

Yet Michael would have none of that. Despite his wife's agonized screams to leave the child alone since she was clearly dead, the father tried unsuccessfully to revive Lizzie, punching her chest repeatedly. Twenty minutes passed, and out of desperation for his daughter's life, Michael started to command the spirit of death to leave the girl's body.

"I command the spirit of death to leave this body!" Michael repeatedly cried out. "Elizabeth, I command your spirit to come back!"

Officers and paramedics arrived on the scene, but out of respect for the father's grief and due to the intensity of his shouting, they all decided to wait a little longer before they tried to take the girl's body away.

Forty minutes passed from the time Michael first had found the body, when suddenly Lizzie started to cough out water. The paramedics stared in disbelief as the father held his girl tightly against his chest, crying and thanking God for this miracle.

Bernardo's Story

A friend of mine, Bernardo, was a prison warden. One day there was a riot, and one of his guards was shot numerous times at close range and died. Bernardo had received an impartation from Randy and was already performing many miracles at this point. When he heard the news that one of his officers had been shot and had died in the ambulance on the way to the hospital, he picked up his Bible and went to see him.

When Bernardo arrived at the hospital, he saw the doctors leaving the guard's room. They were shaking their heads and saying that there was nothing they could do for him. The guard's wife was crying beside her husband's dead body. His heart monitor displayed a flat line.

Bernardo came in, laid his hands on the guard's dead body and prayed out loud: "I command the spirit of death to leave, and I command the spirit of life back into him!"

As he did this, the guard inhaled a deep breath, and the heart monitor started moving and beeping again. The doctors rushed back into the room and then operated on him to take care of his injuries. The guard is now alive and well.

Death Is Not Invincible

Jesus is the same yesterday, today and forever. All authority was given to Him, and He conquered the last enemy, death, on the cross. As Christians, we have to dispel the belief that death is an undefeatable enemy, and we have to make praying for the dead a common feature of the Christian lifestyle. I always preach this at our church here in Rio, Brazil, and our disciples are always looking for opportunities to lay hands on the dead. They attend every funeral they can and pray for the deceased. They fully believe that one of these days a whole town will be saved because they will see that Jesus still has power over death.

I want to encourage you to join us and pray for the dead. You don't have to go to the funeral of complete strangers, but don't miss an opportunity to pray for the dead to be raised, as the Lord leads you.

Remember the testimonies I shared here. Remember the Bible passages where Jesus and the disciples raised the dead. Remember that Jesus Himself commissioned us and told us to raise the dead.

Stay filled with the Holy Spirit and connected with God. Jesus hates death so much that His grave was borrowed. He knew He would only stay in it for a couple of days. God hates death and has given you and me authority over it. Go, therefore, and raise the dead in Jesus' name!

Prayer to Raise the Dead

Among many great lessons I have learned in my life, here is a very valuable one: If you want to climb a mountain, find someone who has been there and ask that person how he or she did it. Jesus has healed the sick, and He is always our best model. How did Jesus pray to heal the sick or raise the dead? He gave words of command. Short prayers. It is not because of how long or how loud we pray that we will be heard. God is not deaf; we don't have to shout. And we don't have to pray long prayers, either, for He knows what we will say before the thought comes into our heart (see Psalm 139:4). Keeping those things in mind, these are the steps my disciples and I take when praying for the dead to be raised:

1. We stay away from sin in our heart, mind and actions. Sinning gives the devil ammunition against us and sucks our confidence, boldness and authority away.
2. We stay connected to the Holy Spirit.
3. We try to get to the deceased person as soon as possible. For our faith's sake, it is better to pray for the dead before they are embalmed.
4. As much as possible, we try to get other people out of the room where we will be praying (except for parents or spouses).
5. We lay hands on the dead body (usually on the shoulders or feet) and pray short words of command.

Our short prayer of command, in which we quote the Word of God (specifically Romans 8:2 NASB), goes something like this:

In the name and authority of Jesus Christ, we command the spirit of death to leave, "for the law of the Spirit of life in Christ Jesus has set you free from the law of sin and death."

We may repeat this prayer up to three times while laying hands on the body. Of course, we are always seeking the direction of the Holy Spirit. Sometimes He may lead us to pray differently, but the prayers are always short and we always follow His lead.

I talked earlier in this chapter about how to know if it is God's will for you to raise someone from the dead or not. You have to stay in alignment with His will. Using your discernment, it will not take long for you to notice if the Holy Spirit is in the situation or not. When He is moving, He will tell you what to do. You will feel His presence, and He will guide you.

For example, if my team and I pray two or three times and nothing happens with the deceased person, we will start getting ready to leave. If we see signs that the Holy Spirit is moving, however, such as the eyelids fluttering or the body getting warm, we will persist a little longer. If nothing more happens after a while, we will hug the family members and console them with words of love and comfort. We try at that point to help prepare their hearts for the grieving process.

If the deceased person does get raised from the dead, though, the first thing to do is bring him or her something to eat and some water. That is what Jesus did when He raised Jairus's daughter from the dead (Mark 5:41–43).

There have been hundreds of cases of people raised from the dead in the name of Jesus. We are living in the days of the last harvest, and the Holy Spirit is releasing His power on a generation of Moseses and Elijahs who will perform mighty signs and wonders, confirming the Word of God with demonstrations of power (Revelation 11:3–6; 15:3). Yet for many of us living in these amazing times, the tendency is to drop "raise the dead" right out of the list of things Jesus commanded us to do in Matthew 10:8, "Heal the sick, raise the dead, cleanse those who have leprosy, drive out demons." Yet it is a vital demonstration of the message that He told us to proclaim: "The kingdom of heaven is at hand" (Matthew 10:7 NKJV).

6

Miracles

But Jesus looked at them and said to them, "With men this
is impossible, but with God all things are possible."

Matthew 19:26 NKJV

What is the difference between a healing and a miracle? Basically, a healing is any restoration of health. It can occur instantly or over time, and it can happen by God's power or by human methods. A miracle also can occur instantly or over time, but it can only take place by divine intervention. For instance, if a man has a cataract on his left eye, he can have his vision restored through conventional means like surgery. That would be a healing. If the man is instantly healed after a prayer, however, then that would be a healing and a miracle.

What is the difference between a healing and a miracle? The dictionary defines *healing* as "the process of making or becoming sound or healthy again: the gift of healing."[1] It defines *miracle* as "a surprising and welcome event that is not explicable by natural or scientific laws and is therefore considered to be the work of a divine agency: the miracle of rising from the grave."[2]

By those definitions, a healing is when someone's recovery from a sickness could have been attained by normal methods such as medical treatment or the improvement of the immunological system. A miracle, however, is something that could not have been attained by natural means. A miracle does not happen by natural means; it is a recovery that can only have happened by divine intervention. The distinction between the two, then, is that a healing can come through natural means, whereas a miracle can come only through divine means.

Here are two examples from Scripture that will help us better understand that distinction. One is a healing, the other a miracle. At Capernaum, Peter's mother-in-law was sick with a fever (see Matthew 8:14–15; Mark 1:29–31; Luke 4:38–39). Jesus healed her supernaturally, but could her fever have been healed by natural means—herbs, teas, medical treatment or an improved immunological system? Yes, a healing could have come through natural means, so this instance is called a healing.

In the other instance, Jesus passed by a man born blind and stopped to restore his sight (see John 9:1–12). Could any natural means—herbs, teas, medical treatment or an improved immunological system—have healed the man's eyes? No. Even today, more than two thousand years later, nothing and no one in the medical field can restore sight to the blind, especially to someone with congenital visual impairment. This instance was a miracle.

Mark makes this distinction between a healing and a miracle when he narrates Jesus' visit to His hometown of Nazareth. Mark's gospel tells us, "He could not do any miracles there, except lay his hands on a few sick people and heal them. He was amazed at their lack of faith" (Mark 6:5–6). So due to their unbelief, Jesus could not perform any miracles in that city, though He did perform a few healings.

The following stories are not just healings; they are miracles—awesome, jaw-dropping miracles—that we have seen God perform through us for His glory.

God Goes Wireless

"All things are possible!" Randy Clark shouted into the microphone. "All you have to do is believe and receive your miracle!"

The night was electric with the presence of God. In the midst of the crowd was a woman who heard Randy's words and believed. She was in her fifties and had long, reddish hair and fair skin. She came to the meeting that night believing for her miracle, and she was ready for it.

Randy told everyone, "Place your hand on your body where you need your miracle, and don't ask—only receive, for He is here to heal you."

When she heard that, this woman believed with all her heart. She placed the palm of her hand over her blind left eye, and God restored her sight. When we encouraged people to come to the front to share their testimonies, she came forward. She told us that she had been blind in her left eye, but now she could see.

"How long had you been blind in that eye?" I asked.

"Five years," she told me. "I had retinal displacement. They did many surgeries on my eye, but they could not save it."

She went on to tell me that the doctors had filled the vitreous cavity of her eye completely with silicone oil to try to fix it, but they still could not do so. To make matters worse, the eye would not stay in the socket. It would fall out, so they surgically disconnected the eyeball from the optical nerve and braced it with a silicone strap to keep it in the socket. In other words, her eye was no longer connected to her brain. The doctors said she would never see out of that eye again, but she believed the truth—that nothing is impossible for God.

"So during the time of prayer you covered your eye with your hand, and when you took your hand off, you could see?" I asked.

"Yes," she said, smiling.

"Okay, cover your right eye," I told her, "and tell me how many fingers I'm showing you."

She covered her right eye and looked at my hand with the eye that had been blind. I showed her some fingers, and she got the number right every time. We high-fived each other and celebrated that incredible miracle.

Later that night, when we were having our staff meeting, we were marveling about all the healings and miracles we had seen.

"You know, guys," I told the staff, "I know all things are possible, but this silicone eye one is driving me crazy. I can't stop wondering how it's possible for her to see out of that eye since the optical nerve has been cut off and the eye is not even connected to the brain."

There was a moment of silence, and then one of our young interns raised his index finger and said with a smile, "It's wireless!"

Later on, we went back to that same church. The same woman came to us with test results showing that her eye had miraculously healed and that she now had a brand-new optical nerve. This is the second case I have seen of a creative miracle resulting in a brand-new optical nerve. That which we call a miracle, the doctors call spontaneous remission.

A Punch and a Healing

I was ministering once at a church near Cincinnati, Ohio. The presence of God was intense as I shared with the crowd some wonderful healing stories we have witnessed over the years. At the end I invited those who would like to receive prayer to the front. Many people came up and received healing. One lady had had surgery on her left foot, and she could not walk normally or run. After we prayed, she walked and ran without any problem for the first time in years.

Two amazing miracles happened to a young man named Paul and his wife, Whitney. The wife was battling a bacterial infection called chronic Lyme disease. I prayed for her and the Holy Spirit touched her, causing her to fall back into the arms of the catcher behind her. She was totally healed.

The husband did not receive a healing; he received a miracle. Crohn's disease and colitis were killing off his digestive system, and he had already had almost all his intestines surgically removed. After eight surgeries, the doctors said that he did not have enough of his intestines or bowel left to function normally. They told him that he would not be able to live apart from having a permanent feeding tube.

Both Paul and Whitney had reached a point where they figured these illnesses would reign in their lives, and then a couple of friends invited them to the service that night. They came, and although they were weary and a little uncomfortable with the atmosphere that was new to them, they began to hope again when the Holy Spirit started to confirm in their hearts that He was indeed moving in that place.

When Paul came up to me for prayer and explained his condition to me, I heard the Holy Spirit say, *Punch him.*

You gotta be kidding me, right? I asked the Holy Spirit. *My name is not Smith Wigglesworth.*

Punch him hard, I heard again, *right in the lower abdomen.*

God, I prayed silently, *I'm not in Brazil. This is America. If I punch him and he isn't healed, he can and probably will sue me. Worse than that, what if I punch him and he dies? Then I'll go to jail!*

Punch him, I heard again.

Now, I thank God that Randy Clark has mentored me, because besides many other important principles, I learned this one precious lesson from him: People may not always be healed, but they must always be loved. I did not see how I could be loving and gentle while punching Paul, but it occurred to me that I could at least tell him what I was about to do before I did it and get his permission.

I said, "Mister, I'm sorry, but I believe the Lord just told me to punch you in the abdomen so you can be healed."

To my surprise, he said, "Okay, go ahead," with an excited smile.

This was a brand-new experience for me. This was the first time in my life that I had told a guy, "Hey, I'm going to punch you in the guts," and the guy had said with a smile, "Okay, go ahead."

After getting his permission, I had an usher stand behind him, just in case. Fearfully but obediently, I punched Paul in the gut. When I did, the word *"Fire!"* came out of my mouth in a loud scream. I punched really hard, too. (Later, Paul told me he had felt his intestines move inside when I punched him.) The power released over him was so intense that he fell back on top of his catcher, and both ended up shaking under the power on the floor.

I have to be honest with you, that one scared me. Nevertheless, I have learned that it is okay to be afraid, but it is not okay to be disobedient. I was afraid but obedient, and God honored that. A little while later I got an email from that couple telling me that Whitney was totally healed. The Lyme disease had completely disappeared from her body. And Paul's intestines had miraculously grown much longer, an impossibility in the natural. When the doctors operated on him again, they were able to reconnect his digestive tract using the new growth.

Unusual Approaches to Healing

Spitting, shouting, jumping or punching people is not new in charismatic circles. We have accounts of preachers like Smith

Wigglesworth, a faith hero to an entire generation, who would violently punch people, and they would be healed. Wigglesworth was known as an apostle of faith. Miracles and healings were common in his meetings. A famous and unusual healing happened on a certain occasion when a man with stomach cancer came forward for prayer. He was in terrible shape and in a lot of pain. Commanding the pain to be gone, Wigglesworth punched the man right in the stomach. He punched him so hard that he sent the man halfway across the room.

As the man lay there motionless on the floor, many of his relatives started shouting, "You killed him! He's dead!"

Wigglesworth replied, "He's healed!"

A few minutes went by, and the man finally rose up, completely healed. This kind of unusual healing happened more than once in Wigglesworth's ministry.[3]

We do have a biblical basis for unusual approaches to healing. On three different occasions Jesus used spit to heal the sick (see Mark 7:33; 8:23; John 9:6). I can picture Jesus, the incarnation of love, applying the spit with the tenderness of a mother applying ointment to her wounded child. In fact, that is how the blind man felt. When they asked him how he had gotten healed, he did not say that Jesus put spit or mud on his eyes. He said, "The man called Jesus made mud and anointed my eyes and said to me, 'Go to Siloam and wash.' So I went and washed and received my sight" (John 9:11 ESV). He used the word *anointed* to describe what Jesus did to him. I cannot help but think that Jesus so lovingly applied the mud that the blind man felt as though Jesus had applied the most precious myrrh to his eyes.

God has prompted me to pray with unusual approaches quite often, even though I am not always comfortable with them. After all, as John Wimber would always say, faith is spelled R-I-S-K. Whenever I do something unusual, however,

I control the urge to go ahead and do it right away. I first turn to the person who has come forward, and in a loving, fatherly way I share with them what I feel led to do. If they agree, I will proceed, but not before making sure I have a catcher or any other requirement in place to assure the person's safety. Above all, I will only do something unusual if I am certain it is from the Father. I will not proceed if I have the slightest doubt in my mind, unless it simply involves giving a word of knowledge. I give out a word of knowledge at the slightest impression that it may be from God, but that is because there is very little danger involved.

No matter what your ministry is and how you are called to execute it, if you are not motivated by love, you are not motivated by God. If God does not motivate your ministry, He is not leading it. If God is not in leading your ministry, then who is? If love is a force, then it is the most powerful force in the universe, because God is love. But God is not a force. He is a person. He was already a person before Jesus' incarnation as the Christ, before He experienced what it is to be human. If God is love and if God is a person, then love is a person. As children of God, we should also be the incarnation of love. Love should come forth from us through our language and actions, and through how we respond to people who interact with us on a daily basis. If we are not led by love, then we are not led by God.

Keys for a Faith-Filled Atmosphere

God wants to release His healing, miracle-working power over you. Jesus has already paid the price for you to receive His power, and His desire is to see you benefit from it. The Kingdom is yours, but owning it and being able to access it are two different stories. You can compare it to forgetting your keys and being locked out of your home. The house is yours, but without the keys you cannot open the door and enter it.

Through Jesus Christ, God has made you an heir of the Kingdom, and to the heirs the keys are given. Jesus said, "I will give you the keys of the kingdom of heaven; whatever you bind on earth will be bound in heaven, and whatever you loose on earth will be loosed in heaven" (Matthew 16:19).

There are three key elements to accessing the Kingdom of God in your life—the power of the Word of God, the power of the testimony and worship. These three help create an atmosphere of faith where miracles happen. As you use these keys, you will come into agreement with God and release His anointing so that you can be healed and stay healed.

I talked back in chapter 2 about how the power of the Word of God and the power of testimonies help build people's faith for healing. Here I want to talk just a little more about testimonies, but I also want to address worship. Let's look at that key element first.

Worship

To create an atmosphere of faith, the first key is worship. It is the first and most important thing we can do. We are directed to "fear God and give him glory" and to "worship him who made the heavens, the earth, the sea and the springs of water" (Revelation 14:7). Worship attracts the presence of God, and if we are to see any healings or miracles take place, we must make sure He has come down. Yes, we carry His presence; we are the present-day Ark of the Covenant. In the Old Testament we see that God gave the people of Israel an Ark that represented His presence among His people. Today, we are the Ark of the Covenant. The presence of God dwells within us, for we are temples of the Holy Spirit (see 1 Corinthians 6:19).

You may walk in such a deep connection with God that miracles will follow you wherever you go. That is not the case for most believers, however. Most people live their daily lives worrying about their bills, bosses, deadlines and all the other stresses of life. If you identify yourself more with the latter group than with the former, then you must make sure to attract God's presence, and again, the best way to attract His presence is through worship.

When John fell at the feet of the angel who appeared to him on the Isle of Patmos, the angelic being told him not to be afraid because he was only a fellow servant of the Lord. The heavenly being then went on to release this tremendous revelation from heaven: "Worship God! For the testimony of Jesus is the spirit of prophecy" (Revelation 19:10 NKJV). The angel gave John an important insight into understanding the Kingdom: *Worship, together with the testimony of Jesus, unleashes the power of God.*

God allowed the angel to unlock this revelation because God intended—and still intends—to unleash His healing power on the earth through His children. But why exactly did the angel tell John that the testimony of Jesus is the spirit of prophecy? How is that connected to his first statement, to worship God?

These statements are not disconnected at all. John fell at the angel's feet. What is that? Worship. Why did people in those days (and still today) worship a god? To receive favor, gifts, provision, healing and any other human need they had that they could not provide for themselves. If they needed it to rain on their crops, they would worship their god and ask for rain. What was the angel saying? He was essentially saying, "Worship God. Bow before Him. Whatever it is that you need, ask Him in worship, and He will grant it to you."

We can see examples in Scripture of the Lord being drawn by worship. This happened in the Temple:

The trumpeters and musicians joined in unison to give praise and thanks to the LORD. Accompanied by trumpets, cymbals and other instruments, the singers raised their voices in praise to the LORD and sang: "He is good; his love endures forever." Then the temple of the LORD was filled with the cloud.

2 Chronicles 5:13

God has not changed. His presence still shows up where people are worshiping Him.

One time when I was in a crusade with Randy in Brazil, he asked the church to repeat twenty times, "For the Lord is good, and His love endures forever." After the last time, the entire congregation of five thousand people shouted praises at the top of their lungs. The result? Without anyone praying for or laying hands on them, hundreds of people were healed, including dozens who had paralyzed limbs or joints that were unable to move due to failed surgeries and metal implants.

When we open our hearts before God in worship and tear off all our fig leaves of religion, He shows up. When His presence manifests in worship, healing flows naturally from Him. I have been in meetings where the presence of God was so strong during the worship that I did not even have to preach or pray for the sick. All I said was, "God's presence is here to heal you. Don't even ask; just thank Him for your healing and try to do what you could not do before." Immediately, all over the church people would be crying and laughing with joy as they received their miracles.

It has been a couple of decades now, but one time I was working as a translator for Benny Hinn during his healing crusade in a soccer stadium called Portuguesa in São Paulo. The stadium was packed with more than twenty thousand people. Many brought the sick, especially the lame, the crippled, the terminally ill and the paraplegic, and laid them down on the

96

grass of the soccer field in front of the stage. They believed that God would heal the ones they brought, and He did.

As Benny's team filled the stadium with beautiful worship, the presence of God was so strong that the people who stepped in front of the stage struggled to remain standing. The weight of the glory of God pushed them down to their knees, and eventually they were facedown, crying in the presence of God. All over the stadium, thousands of people received healing under Benny's shouts of "Be healed!"

I was kneeling beside an agonized man who had been brought into the stadium on a stretcher. We were all worshiping God, and His presence consumed us with His love. I turned to the family of the man and asked what his ailment was.

"Terminal cancer," said his daughter. "The doctor has given him just a few days to live," she added, tears streaming down her face.

I began to cry, and God's presence and compassion filled my heart to a degree I had never felt before. I laid my hands on the man and prayed for him. I don't know the exact words I said, but I know what happened next had nothing to do with my words.

"Help me up," said the man to his daughter.

She and a couple of other relatives helped him up. In a matter of minutes he was standing up with his hands raised, crying and praising God.

"I'm healed!" he said, crying tears of joy.

I saw him go home carrying his mat, and I felt as if I were inside the book of Acts. I knew that God had heard my prayer and the prayer of hundreds and even thousands of others who received healing that night. Afterward, I could not stop thinking, *Why did they get healed here and not in their homes or in their own churches?* I believe the answer is that the power of God was released by His presence as He came down, drawn by our worship.

Another important aspect of ushering in the Lord's presence through worship is thanksgiving. David often exhorts believers to be grateful to the Lord (see Psalm 28:7; 69:30; 95:2–3), and he even declares that we enter the gates of the Lord through thanksgiving alone (see Psalm 100:4). Paul instructs us to "give thanks in all circumstances; for this is God's will for you in Christ Jesus" (1 Thessalonians 5:18). We must worship God with grateful hearts no matter what situation we are facing, because He is always good.

The Power of the Testimony

The second key to creating an atmosphere of faith where the presence of God will be honored and healings and miracles will take place is to understand *the power of the testimony of Jesus*. We looked at this a little in chapter 2. When the angel told John about the testimony of Jesus being the "spirit of prophecy," he was describing the work of faith that is released in the hearts of those who hear about the works of Jesus. This is why it is so important before you pray to share testimonies of what Jesus has done for others. As those you are about to pray for hear about what Jesus has done for others, they receive a measure of faith from heaven that will cause them to believe for their own miracle.

In other words, when we preach about what Jesus has already done, it creates an atmosphere of faith for those who listen to believe that He will do it again. If we do not preach about the testimony of Jesus, they cannot believe. "How can they believe in the one of whom they have not heard? And how can they hear without someone preaching to them?" (Romans 10:14).

When people's hearts are warmed by the power of the testimony, it creates an atmosphere of faith. We have seen it hundreds, if not thousands, of times. Wherever we minister, we always prepare the hearts of the listeners with testimonies, stories and even videos of healings that have taken place. Wherever we share those things, hundreds of people get healed of the same conditions described in those testimonies.

When I did not know anything about healing, I was often upset that nobody was being healed at our services. Today I know that one of the reasons that nobody was being healed was because nobody was preaching about healing. The church simply did not expect anybody to be healed. People did not believe for their healing because they did not hear a message that stirred up their faith. Paul describes the opposite effect: "Faith comes by hearing, and hearing by the word of God" (Romans 10:17 NKJV).

He Healed Them All

Whether you are seeking your healing or praying for others to be healed, it will do you no good to debate the reasons why people don't get healed. What will help you create miracle-working faith is knowing why and how others received their healing, so you, too, can be healed and become an agent of God's power on earth. A religious spirit focuses on what is wrong; the Spirit of God empowers you to make things right.

Independently of what we know about healing, our message must always be that *Jesus wants everyone healed.* This is the kind of message that creates hope, expectation and faith in people's hearts. Where there is expectation and faith, miracles will take place. Yes, it is true that not everybody who has been prayed for has been healed, but I like to say that not everybody has been healed *yet.* The reason they have not been healed is not in or from God, because God is good and He wants all to be healed. Whatever is preventing you or someone else from getting healed is not on God's side of the equation. It is on our human side. We must identify the factors that create an environment for healing and practice them in our lives.

When Jesus walked on the earth, thousands of people would come to Him afflicted by evil spirits and illnesses, and He healed them all: "When evening came, many who were demon-possessed were brought to him, and he drove out the spirits with a word and healed all the sick" (Matthew 8:16). Pay attention to this part of the verse: "and healed all the sick." How many did He heal? That's right—all of them. Nobody went back home without their healing.

Someone may think, *That was fine for Jesus, but no one else has been able to do that.*

Actually, Jesus' disciples had that kind of track record after His ascension: "Crowds gathered also from the towns around Jerusalem, bringing their sick and those tormented by impure spirits, and all of them were healed" (Acts 5:16). Those healings were performed by Christians, not by the Christ. The followers of Jesus were healing all who were sick, and even today there are disciples of Jesus laying hands on the sick and healing them.

Before you pray for the sick, it is vitally important that you lay a solid biblical foundation for the fact that healing is for today. The Holy Spirit will open up the ears of the people, and they will believe. If you want people to be healed, you must make sure you share the testimonies of what Jesus has done. Share with them that Jesus is the same today, and that He still heals the sick. Read as many Scriptures about healing as you can. Quote the words of Jesus on the subject and have the congregation read the text with you as you preach about it. Encourage them to expect to receive healing, and stir up their faith with stories and testimonies. Jesus will be faithful and heal. He always does.

If you are the one who needs healing, then read as many Scriptures as you can about it. Listen to messages on healing and read books about it. Talk to people who were healed, especially those who had the same condition you have. Interview them and ask them to give you details. Did they feel the presence of God? What was it like? Where were they? Did someone pray for them, or were they sovereignly healed? I am sure that as they share their testimonies, you will notice there is an atmosphere of faith around them. Building an atmosphere of faith draws the presence of God and His power to heal.

The Laying On of Hands

Though the laying on of hands is not necessarily an unusual approach to healing in modern Christian circles, somehow for centuries the Church has neglected and undermined this practice when it comes to healing. Yet this was the method Jesus often implemented in His ministry to bless and heal (see Matthew 19:13–15; Mark 6:5; 8:23–25). Many New Testament passages clearly show Jesus and His disciples laying hands on the sick and praying for them to be healed. When Jairus came to Jesus in order that his daughter would be healed and live, he begged, "Come and lay your hands on her, that she may be healed" (Mark 5:23 NKJV).

The Church must learn and practice this fundamental teaching. It is a basic style of prayer and a prophetic promise Jesus gave for those who believe: "They will lay hands on the sick, and they will recover" (Mark 16:18 NKJV). Once I learned and understood that this is how God heals, I never prayed for the sick without the laying on of hands. For me, praying for the sick without doing this is like trying to row a boat without any paddles.

All things are possible for God. Whether it is growing out part of your body like a missing limb, an intestine or an optical nerve, there are no healings or miracles too hard for God. If you have faith, then (in the words of the popular song title) there really "ain't no mountain high enough" for God.

Whatever it is that you need, ask God and believe, and it will happen for you. As Jesus declared, "Therefore I tell you, whatever you ask for in prayer, believe that you have received it, and it will be yours" (Mark 11:24). And above all, remember this: People may not always be healed, but they must always be loved!

PART TWO

Hindrances to Healing

7

The Issue of Sin

See, you are well again. Stop sinning or something worse
may happen to you.

John 5:14

Many people come to us complaining that a few days after they
got healed, their condition came back and they got sick again.
They come to ask why they lost their healing. I had a pastor of
a large church come to me after a crusade to say that a couple
from his church were very upset because they had been healed in
our meeting, but a few days later their sicknesses came back even
worse than before. They said they did not believe our ministry
was from God, because had it really been from God, they would
not have become sick again. The pastor asked me what I thought.

My answer to him was simple: If people go back to whatever caused their sicknesses in the first place, they surely will
be sick again.

Sadly, it is not uncommon to have people get healed and
then, after a while, go back to being sick again. This happens

based on the origin of the sickness. Depending on what caused the sickness in the first place, the condition may return after a healing takes place.

The Cause of Sickness

In ancient Jewish culture based on the Law of Moses, sin was the cause of sickness, disease and death. Yet the Jews also believed that a child would not pay for the sins of his or her parents. A man blind from birth was therefore a challenge to their belief system. This is why, when the disciples saw a blind man by the road, they asked Jesus, "Rabbi, who sinned, this man or his parents, that he was born blind?" (John 9:2).

Before man sinned in the Garden of Eden, there was no sickness. The first sin in the Garden opened the door for sickness, disease and death to enter our world. And as the apostle Paul said, "The wages of sin is death" (Romans 6:23), so the disciples' question to Jesus was—and is—very relevant. Since the man was blind from the moment he was born, his blindness could not have resulted from his own sin. The disciples therefore assumed that since sickness was a result of sin and he had not sinned, obviously it must have been his parents who had sinned and caused him to be born blind. But this also posed a problem for their theology, as the Law also stated that children would not bear the sins of their parents: "The son shall not suffer for the iniquity of the father" (Ezekiel 18:20 ESV).

The disciples were confused, and even the religious authorities did not have an answer for their question. They came to Jesus, hoping He would give them an answer for the terrible riddle.

Jesus' answer is interesting: "Neither this man nor his parents sinned, but that the works of God should be revealed in him" (John 9:3 NKJV). We know Jesus was not saying that none of them had ever sinned, because we know "all have sinned and fall short of the glory of God" (Romans 3:23). Jesus was simply answering the disciples' question regarding whose sin caused this man's blindness. His answer was that it was neither the man's sin nor that of his parents.

Yet when Jesus answered that the man was born blind so that God's works might be revealed in him, what was He saying? Let's look at that more closely. Was He saying that God had made the man blind from birth so that He could reveal His power through him? I don't think so. First of all, we know that no evil comes from God. Rather, "Every good gift and every perfect gift is from above, and comes down from the Father of lights" (James 1:17 NKJV). God did not put blindness in that man when he was born.

Then what is Jesus saying here? Let's read the text more fully in another translation:

> Jesus answered, "It was not that this man sinned, or his parents, but that the works of God might be displayed in him. We must work the works of him who sent me while it is day; night is coming, when no one can work."
>
> John 9:3–4 ESV

As you may already know, there are no commas or periods in the Greek language. Most of the English translations we have of the Bible place the punctuation marks where the translators thought they made the most sense. But in this case, look what happens when we change the punctuation marks in the text:

> Jesus answered, "It was not that this man sinned, or his parents, but that the works of God might be displayed in him we must work the works of him who sent me while it is day; night is coming, when no one can work."

Did you notice the difference? Look again: "That the works of God might be displayed in him we must work the works of him who sent me." The answer Jesus gave the disciples was clear: That the works of God might be made manifest in the sick, we must work the works of the Father. From this we can see that it was neither the man's sin nor his parents' sin that caused his blindness, and that we must heal the sick so that the works of God might be displayed.

So Jesus did not say, "This happened so that God's work might be revealed in him." Rather, Jesus said, "That the works of God might be displayed in him we must work the works of him who sent me."

Why is this important? Actually, it more than important—it is crucial. If Jesus had said that the man was born blind so that God's works could be displayed in him, then it would mean that we are serving a self-centered, sadistic God who has no consideration for the suffering of the broken. But this is not the God we serve. God is a loving, caring Father. That man was not born blind so that Jesus could show off. No! That man was born blind. Period. It was nobody's fault or sin in particular that caused him to be born blind; it was the result of the fallen world in which we live—the result of the bad choice made back in the Garden, which opened the door to sickness, disease and death.

Here is what Jesus' answer meant: "It will do this blind man no good to know whose sin caused his blindness. What will make a difference to him is to know that God the Father has sent Me to be the Light of the world and to drive away all the darkness caused by sin. In order for the works of the Father to be made manifest in this blind man, we must work while I am around, because I am the Light of the world."

The disciples focused on the origin of the sickness; Jesus focused on putting an end to the sickness. Contaminated by the yeast of the Pharisees—the spirit of religion—the disciples had set their minds on something lifeless and pointless. Jesus set His focus on displaying the love and power of the Father.

Religion without the manifestation of the love and power of God through miracles is empty. This is what the Pharisees had practiced for centuries, an empty religion, and they used it to control the population and remain in power. Long, empty speeches, doctrines, sermons, texts and rituals mean nothing if there is no demonstration of God's love and power through healing. Anyone who claims to be from God and does not demonstrate God's power through acts of compassion, signs, wonders, healings and miracles is not a complete representation of the Father. Jesus is our model, and He said, "Very truly I tell you, whoever believes in me will do the works I have been doing, and they will do even greater things than these, because I am going to the Father" (John 14:12).

What is at the core of His answer? *Don't waste your energy trying to figure out where the darkness comes from; just let the light shine.* Instead of trying to figure out what caused someone's problem, let's allow God's light to shine through us over them and bring them healing. Jesus saw this blind man as an opportunity to fulfill the Father's calling on His life, which was to destroy the works of the devil: "For this purpose the Son of God was manifested, that He might destroy the works of the devil" (1 John 3:8 NKJV).

What matters most for us as the children of God is that we see sickness not as an opportunity to debate theology, but rather as an opportunity to undo the works of the devil and do the works of the Father by bringing healing and light to a generation of people who suffer in darkness.

Sin No More

We know that before sin entered the world, there was no sickness, no disease and no death. We also know that a sinful lifestyle will lead to sickness, disease and even death.

109

For example, if someone smokes all his life and then at a certain point contracts emphysema, it was obviously his sin (in this case an addiction to tobacco, and any addiction is sin) that caused his sickness and could eventually cause his death. If someone lives an immoral lifestyle and contracts a sexually transmitted disease, again, his condition is a result of his sin. There are also other less obvious sins, and for each sin there is a different consequence.

In John 5 Jesus heals a man who could not walk for thirty-eight years. After healing the man, Jesus warns him that sin can open the door to sickness: "See, you are well again. Stop sinning or something worse may happen to you" (verse 14). In this passage we have an important revelation straight from Jesus. What the Lord is saying here is that, clearly, sin causes sickness.

Sin opens the door to sickness in our lives. Sin separates us from God and from all the goodness that comes from Him. If, after receiving healing, a man goes back to his old ways and gives himself back to sin, then he is distancing himself from God, the source of healing. The result of doing that is sickness. The way around it is to stay connected with God and sin no more.

But can we sin no more? Is it humanly possible not to sin? Yes, it is. Otherwise, Jesus would not have told that man not to sin anymore. Jesus would not tell us to do something that we could not do.

The Intent of the Heart

To understand what it means to "sin no more," we need to differentiate between a sinner and a saint. What is the main difference between the two? *Intent!* The intent of the heart is what separates a sinner from a saint. Jesus taught us this in the parable of the Pharisee and the tax collector:

Two men went up to the temple to pray, one a Pharisee and the other a tax collector. The Pharisee stood by himself and prayed, "God, I thank you that I am not like other people—robbers, evildoers, adulterers—or even like this tax collector. I fast twice a week and give a tenth of all I get."

But the tax collector stood at a distance. He would not look up to heaven, but beat his breast and said, 'God, have mercy on me, a sinner."

I tell you that this man, rather than the other, went home justified before God.

Luke 18:10–14

In the eyes of God, both the Pharisee and the tax collector were sinners. Then what caused the tax collector to be justified rather than the Pharisee? The intent of his heart. The Pharisee did not even recognize that he needed to be justified. He thought he was doing a pretty good job staying righteous and that all he needed to do was make sure that God knew it, too. The tax collector, however, repented and cried out to God for mercy.

If you were guilty of a sin under the Old Covenant, it meant that you had physically committed that sin and would be punished for it if you were caught. But unlike the Old Covenant, where you were considered a sinner when you committed a wrong deed, the New Covenant defines you as committing a sin when you even think about it: "You have heard that it was said, 'You shall not commit adultery.' But I say to you that everyone who looks at a woman with lustful intent has already committed adultery with her in his heart" (Matthew 5:27–28 ESV).

The intent of our heart is what separates sinners from saints. Does that mean we are free to sin as long as we did not intend to do it and we repent afterward? Of course not! That is as foolish as it gets. Sin ultimately leads us away from God and opens the door for sickness to come into our lives. Yet we know that we are born into sin because of Adam's decision in the Garden of

Eden, and that the wages of sin is death. We also know that "if we say we have not sinned, we make him a liar, and his word is not in us" (1 John 1:10 ESV).

If we must all admit that we sin, then why would we not consider ourselves sinners? What is the difference between a sinner and a saint? Putting it simply, sinners spend their lives trying to sin, while saints spend their lives trying not to sin. Sinners seek sin. Saints seek God's face, and as we get closer to God, we get farther from sin. Human nature is driven toward sin; the divine nature is driven away from it.

In the beginning of this chapter I stated that those who, after being healed, go back to the practice or behavior that caused their sickness in the first place will surely be sick again. That is one of the reasons people lose their healing. The opposite is also true. If they repent of their sin and start to seek God's face, they distance themselves from sin and any resulting sickness, and they keep their healing.

Staying close to God helps us both be healed and stay healed. Let's cover ourselves with His divine nature and be filled, baptized and immersed in the Spirit of God so that we may die to sin and live for God (see Romans 6:11).

8

Demonic Affliction

> While they were going out, a man who was demon-possessed
> and could not talk was brought to Jesus. And when the demon
> was driven out, the man who had been mute spoke.
>
> Matthew 9:32–33

There are sicknesses caused by demons. Those who are slaves to
sin open their lives to demonic affliction. Throughout Scripture
we have examples of demons causing muteness, demons causing blindness, demons causing seizures, demons causing flesh
wounds and mad behavior, demons causing physical deformity
and even demons physically wounding people (see Matthew
9:32; 12:22; 17:15; Mark 5:2–5; Luke 11:14; 13:11; Acts 19:16).
We also have numerous examples of Jesus delivering those who
were oppressed by the devil and healing them: "God anointed
Jesus of Nazareth with the Holy Spirit and with power. He
went about doing good and healing all who were oppressed by
the devil, for God was with him" (Acts 10:38 ESV).

Let me quickly point out the difference between demonic possession and demonic oppression—Jesus dealt with both. Demonic possession is the final stage of demonic oppression. Demons start out by oppressing people, and then that oppression may escalate into possession, depending on the level of influence people allow the evil spirit or spirits to have over their lives.

I have prayed for many people with sicknesses and diseases caused by evil spirits, but perhaps the most interesting case was a four-year-old boy who was not only sick but was also demon possessed. I was ministering with Randy Clark in a healing crusade in Brazil on a Sunday night. The meeting was packed with well over four thousand people, and many had come because they had heard about the service from a friend or relative who had received healing during the two previous nights. We had close to one hundred people on our ministry team, but that was not nearly enough to pray for the multitude of people who came to the front every night to receive prayer.

After praying for a few dozen people on this particular night, I took a break and went to the snack room in the back of the building for a coffee refill. When you are in a healing crusade with Randy in Brazil, you need coffee like a race car needs fuel, and it was time for my pit stop. As I was leaving the snack room, a man holding a boy in his arms walked up to me.

"Please help me, Pastor," the man pleaded. As soon as the boy saw me, he started to convulse and scream like a factory siren.

"What's going on?" I asked.

"This is my son. He's being tormented by evil spirits that constantly cause him to be sick," the father explained.

"Since when?" I asked, still holding my coffee jug in my hand.

"Since he was born."

"And how old is he now?"

"He's four." The father tried to hold his son still, while the boy screamed and wailed out of control.

"Okay." I put my coffee down on a table next to us. "Don't worry. Whatever is tormenting your son is going to come out." Being a pastor in Brazil, I get to do a lot of deliverances, especially in churches near the projects or the heavily populated *favelas*, which are informal settlements of substandard housing within larger urban areas.[1] I have prayed for the deliverance of demonized people thousands of times. I knew how to get a demon out, so I thought this case would be easy. I was wrong. When I started to pray for the boy, he began to manifest wildly. The child was oppressed before, but as I started to pray, the demon started talking through the boy's mouth.

"Come out in the name of Jesus," I said.

"No. I won't come out! The boy is mine." A low, guttural voice came out through the little boy's mouth.

For a second I felt as if I were in a horror movie. I must confess that it gave me the shivers. Normally I would follow Randy's deliverance method, but this time did not seem "normal" as far as deliverances go. First of all, I could not call the boy to his senses and talk to him because he was just a little boy. Second, he was in a deep state of demonization. Third, I could see in the spirit that the demon was coming out of the boy when I told him to, but was jumping right back in and tormenting the boy once I finished talking. I knew there was more to this situation than just a simple case of possession.

Knowing Who You Are

I will get back to the boy's story in a minute, but first I want to say that if you are a son or daughter of God, washed and redeemed by His blood, you are royalty. You are the child of the King of kings. Deliverance is not about knowing the right words to say; it is not about a method. It is about knowing who you are. Don't get me wrong—methods are good and helpful.

But it is not the method that makes a demon subject to you. It is the authority you have in knowing who you are in Christ that will drive out the demon.

A good example of spiritual authority, or in this case the lack of authority, can be found in Acts 19, which tells about a Jewish chief priest in Jerusalem by the name of Sceva. He had seven sons, and I imagine that growing up with a father so deeply involved in the things of God, his sons had a natural interest in the supernatural. I can picture these boys following the apostles around and watching what they did and how they exercised authority over the demon possessed.

In those days, religion and the supernatural not only fascinated the Jewish people; it ruled their world. This was a nation founded by a supernatural God, whose founding fathers had often had encounters with God and angels. The priest's young sons started to go around like the apostles, commanding demons to leave in the name of Jesus. The only problem: They did not actually know Jesus. They had never followed Him. They had not given their lives to Him. They had only watched Paul deliver people using Jesus' name, so they decided to mimic Paul.

Authority in the spiritual world, however, does not come by what you know, but by whom you know. Jesus is not a force. He is not a good luck charm. God is a person, just like you and me. He has feelings, He has emotions, He loves, He hates. He knows those who love Him and those who don't. This was Sceva's sons' mistake. They thought that using the name of Jesus alone had the power and authority over the demonic realm. As a consequence, the demon tore off their clothes, beat them up and sent them all running for their lives (see Acts 19:11–20).

Spiritual authority comes only through relationship and intimacy with God the Father, in Christ Jesus, through the Holy Spirit. If you don't have that relationship, then you don't have spiritual authority. Those who think they do are only being deceived by the same spirits they believe are under their control. Authority must have the support of heaven, or else it will crumble down. Jesus had authority on the earth because He only did the Father's will. Because of this submission, Jesus had the Father's support. If you walk in relationship and submission to the Father, then you will have His support, too, and His support gives you spiritual authority.

Deliverance and Salvation

Back to the story: So there I was in front of the snack room with this father and his demonized four-year-old son. The boy was wreaking havoc in his father's arms and my coffee was getting cold, so I had a personal reason to be mad at this demon.

"Get ahold of your boy!" I instructed the father.

"I can't!" the father cried out, totally dazed and disoriented.

"What's your name?" I asked.

"Anthony," the man said, struggling to keep his boy still. "My name is Anthony."

"Okay, Anthony, I'm glad you came to me. Now, you must control your boy, okay?" I spoke firmly yet calmly with him. "He's just a four-year-old. How old are you?"

"I'm thirty."

"Well, how is it you cannot control a little boy?"

"He's stronger than me!"

The father began to cry as the boy on his lap wriggled frantically, like a fish trying to jump back into the water. Then I saw something I had never seen before. The boy crawled around the father's upper body like a spider would crawl around a stick. That really made me feel as if I were in a horror movie!

"In the name of Jesus," I began again, pointing my index finger at the demon, "I command you to stay still."

The boy immediately became still, but he would not stop wailing, whimpering and crying. Obviously that foul spirit was tormenting him, and I could not have any more of that. Three times I commanded the demon to leave the boy, and all three times I saw the lizard-like demon come out and then jump right back in the boy, laughing at me. After the third time, I told the demon to come out, but it pulled out a key chain, wiggled it at me, laughed a horrible, unnerving laugh and jumped back into the little boy again.

What's going on? I thought. I had never experienced a demon's disdain for me like this. I had only seen them leave on the first command. I knew that in order for this deliverance to be successful, I needed the Father's help. I have learned never to do anything in my own strength. I always remain totally dependent on God.

I called Daddy for help, saying under my breath, *Father, what is going on?*

He has the keys, Father God told me. *He has been given the right to possess him.*

But he's just a little boy, Father God, I replied in my spirit. *How did this foul spirit get those keys?*

As soon as I asked, Father God showed me a picture. I saw the boy's mother and father holding the boy when he was just a baby. They were dressed in white and surrounded by people playing different types of drums. Someone cut a goat's throat and poured the blood in a bowl. Then an elderly person with white hair came and poured the blood over the baby's head. Along with the vision came discernment about the whole affair.

By this point in my life I had learned that God is love and without Him I can do nothing. With that in mind, I looked gently to the father of the demonized boy, and instead of raising my index finger and saying with a stern voice, "Thus says the Lord," I simply asked, "When the boy was a baby, did you happen to have any involvement with, let's say, any sort of witchcraft?"

The father nodded, biting his lower lip. "Yes."

"Did they happen to wash the baby's head with goat's blood?"

"Yes, they did," he mumbled.

"Was the boy's mother with you on that day?"

"I didn't want to do it," he sobbed, "but she made me."

"Where is she?"

"She's at home." Tears ran down his eyes as he explained, "She wouldn't come to church with me."

"I need you to pay attention to me, okay?" I told the man. "This is *very* important. You and your wife are the legal authorities over this boy. The moment you participated in that ritual with the boy, you consecrated his life to evil spirits. Do you understand?"

"Yes, Pastor Ed, I know that now. I gave my life to Jesus on the first day of this crusade, and that's when my son got sick with a high fever and broke out in sores. Now I know the demons fooled me," he sobbed. "They want to kill my boy."

"Yes, they do," I said, looking him straight in the eye. "But don't you worry, they won't do it, because Jesus is greater. Repeat after me."

As soon as I said, "Repeat after me: Jesus is greater," the demon went crazy. I thought it was already giving us trouble before, but then the boy struggled and screamed so much that the father could barely keep the boy in his arms.

"Anthony, look at me. Focus on what I'm saying," I said as calmly as I could. "I renounce . . ."

"No!" the demon screamed through the boy's throat.

"Do it, Anthony," I continued. "Just repeat after me."

I could tell Anthony was scared, but phrase by phrase he repeated my prayer, renouncing all involvement with witchcraft at the Macumba center where the ritual had taken place.

(Macumba is a religious cult of African origins practiced in Brazil; it is characterized by witchcraft, sorcery and ritual dances.) Then we took back authority over the boy's soul and handed the keys of authority to Jesus.

The whole prayer did not last more than a minute, and by the time we were done, the little boy was peacefully resting his head on his father's shoulder. Standing beside them was an angry demon that had just been evicted from his former home. He did not look happy at all.

I told Anthony how important it was that he bring his wife to church so she could give her life to the Lord and also renounce Macumba. Or else, I warned him, seven demons worse than the first one would come and have their way with his boy (see Matthew 12:43–45). I did not intend to scare him; I was only warning him of the truth.

Anthony went home and brought his wife back to the meeting. By the end of the service that night, both he and his wife had come to the stage to give their lives to Christ. When I saw the two of them standing there, I made sure the wife looked at me when I had everyone repeat the sinner's prayer. With tear-filled eyes she confessed Jesus as Lord over her life. That night not only deliverance but also salvation came to that family.

Discernment Is Key

As with any case concerning sickness, discernment is key. It is important to know that the devil does cause sickness, but it is just as important to know that not every sickness is caused by the devil. If a teenage boy attempts to jump off the roof of his house on his bike and breaks his leg, that is not a spirit of infirmity, that is the spirit of stupid.

Too many times the devil is blamed for things he never did. He gets far too much undeserved credit. Just because something bad happens does not mean it was because of the devil. If someone works all his life as a coal miner and contracts black lung disease, then that sickness is the result of a natural cause. If someone falls from a motorcycle and breaks his legs, then the fractures are the result of a natural cause. If someone has a strong traumatic experience and manifests a disease as a result, then that condition has a psychosomatic cause.

It is extremely important that you discern the different sources of sickness, especially the difference between natural causes, psychosomatic causes and demonic causes. Discernment could be the key to unlocking your healing or someone else's. Once you have discerned the source of the sickness, then you handle it in different ways:

Natural Causes: If the illness has a natural cause, you use words of command in the name and authority of Jesus to pray for healing by speaking health and wellness into the affected area.

Psychosomatic Causes: Psychosomatic illnesses are caused or aggravated by mental factors such as internal conflict or stress. If an illness has a psychosomatic cause, you help the person identify the emotional or mental source of the illness. Once that source is identified, you must help the person deal with it. In the case of emotions related to unforgiveness, for example, you must encourage the person to release forgiveness. Often, when the person releases forgiveness toward the person who has caused the emotional distress, the symptoms of the illness start to disappear. In some cases all the symptoms immediately disappear; in other cases the healing is gradual.

Spiritual Causes: A demon or afflicting spirit is behind an illness with a spiritual cause. Once you have determined that an illness has a spiritual cause, you must tell the person you are praying for to ask the Holy Spirit what doors he or she opened that allowed the evil spirit to enter into his or her life. Once that is determined, using words of command in the name and authority of Jesus, you must lead the person to renounce one by one any involvement, conscious or unconscious, with any afflicting spirits. The person must command the spirits to leave his or her life, body, mind and soul. It may take a couple of prayers of command for pain associated with a spiritual cause to leave. Sometimes the pain moves from one spot to another. You must continue to use words of command in the name and authority of Jesus, telling the spirit of affliction to leave.[2]

Demonic afflictions have no right to stay when you pray, not because of your methodology or how much you know, but because of who you are—a child of the King—and because of whom you know. Because of your relationship and intimacy with God the Father, in Christ Jesus, through the Holy Spirit, you have spiritual authority with the full support of heaven behind it.

PART THREE

Stay Healed

9

Believe the Word

If you believe, you will receive whatever you ask for in prayer.

Matthew 21:22

So many times we tend to put God in a box. After almost a decade of participating in the revival culture that Randy Clark was so instrumental in ushering in, I did not think I had any boxes I put Him in anymore. But God outdid Himself—or at least my idea of Him—once again. Most of the people in our ministry, myself included, have a good, practical understanding of how a word of knowledge works, especially Randy, who has operated in this gift for over twenty years. But one night in Fortaleza, Brazil, God decided to completely shatter our understanding of how a word of knowledge works.

First, let me quickly define a word of knowledge for you. In our movement and in all the churches connected to the Global Awakening and Revival Alliance ministries, words of knowledge are commonly used for healing. A word of knowledge is a gift of the Spirit listed in 1 Corinthians 12:8. It is specific information that the Holy Spirit gives someone about another person. We see Jesus operating in this gift when He sits at the well in Samaria and tells the woman He meets there that she has had five husbands, and that the man she is with now is not her husband (see John 4:17–18). I received the impartation and stirring up of this gift from Randy. Randy received it from Blaine Cook, whom I now am privileged to have as a dear friend. Blaine was the leader of the Vineyard team that visited Randy's Baptist church early on and set Randy on his path toward his calling and destiny. Blaine received the impartation from Lonnie Frisbee, an important figure in the Jesus Movement in the seventies, as well as from John Wimber, one of the founders of the Vineyard movement.

Words of knowledge can come to you in many ways. You can feel a word, see it, think it, hear it, read it, dream it, experience it, taste it or smell it.[1] The current understanding of how a word of knowledge works is that when people who need healing hear a specific word of knowledge connected to their ailment, it strengthens their faith. For example, if a man at one of our meetings needs his gallbladder healed, someone from our team will get a word of knowledge from the Holy Spirit and declare from the stage, "God is healing someone's gallbladder right now." The man will hear this word and know it is for him, and his faith will rise, leading to his healing. This process is so common in our ministry that we view it as one of the more "normal" ways people are healed.

On that particular night in Fortaleza, we had a team of over one hundred people lined up in front of the stage to give out words of knowledge as they received them from God. I went down the line one by one, as we usually do in these meetings, and held the microphone as each person shared a word of knowledge for the crowd. Our team members called out many illnesses from migraines to cancer, and from arthritis to blindness. Many people in the large audience stood up and waved both hands over their heads as a sign that they had received healing. At the end we asked people who had received a major healing to come forward to share their testimonies with the church. Out of the many wonderful miracles we saw that night, I want to share a miracle that was one of the most meaningful to me.

Healed by Faith

"She was deaf from birth," her mother said, still in shock, "and now she can hear. Look, she can hear!"

Obviously, the woman was having a hard time processing what had just happened, which is not an unusual response from someone who has received or witnessed a major miracle. Her daughter was fourteen years old and had never heard a sound in her life. This girl stood there on the stage with us, smiling and looking around, marveling at all the sounds she could now hear.

"How did she receive her healing?" I asked.

"We came to this healing crusade because we have always prayed and believed that one day she would be healed," her mother said, starting to cry. "Then, when a lady on your team gave a word of knowledge about a deaf left ear, our daughter, who was sitting down next to us—bored because she didn't know what was going on—suddenly stood up and started to signal frantically to us that she could hear out of her left ear."

"What was your reaction?" I asked, smiling and excited.

"I don't know. I guess I started asking her what she meant, even though I was believing for her healing. When it actually happened, I didn't know what to think."

"So she received healing in her left ear, correct?"

"Yes."

"And how did she get healed in her right ear?"

"A few minutes after that, a young man on the team said that he felt God was opening the right ear of a young girl. As soon as he said it, my daughter started to freak out and signaled to us that she could hear out of both ears now."

"Okay, let me get this straight. When the first word of knowledge was given for the left ear, her left ear was opened, even though she could not hear the word of knowledge."

"Correct," the mother said, nodding.

"When the second word was given for the right ear, she could now hear it, even though she did not understand the words she was hearing because she had never heard them before. And then she was healed in her right ear."

"That's absolutely right," her mother affirmed.

I turned to Randy, who was just two steps behind me, watching and listening closely to this interview.

"Wow, Randy, what do you think of this?" I asked. "I mean, we always thought a word of knowledge worked by stirring the faith of the person with the illness when he or she *heard* the word, and then that person would receive healing. But here is this girl, who never heard the first word of knowledge and didn't understand the second word, yet she got healed!"

"I don't know," said Randy with a big smile, "but I'm going to have to sit down and think about that one."

We both laughed and started praising God for this amazing miracle. I brought the girl closer to the edge of the platform and politely asked the crowd of three thousand people to be quiet because I wanted to show them what Jesus had done.

I turned to the girl's mother and said, "Tell your daughter in sign language that I'm going to say a word behind her so that she cannot possibly read my lips, and she will hear it through the speakers. Tell her that we understand she has never heard before and therefore cannot speak, but please ask her to repeat the sound she hears as best she can."

The girl's mother agreed and signed my instructions to her daughter. The girl smiled and agreed. I positioned myself behind the girl in front of this excited crowd, and one of the pastors held a microphone to her mouth.

From behind the girl I said clearly and slowly, "Jesus . . . healed . . . me." She repeated the words with a little lisp. The crowd began to cheer, clapping and praising the name of Jesus for the awesome miracle.

If faith comes by hearing the Word of God, and we know that it does, then this girl was not healed because of her faith, for she never heard the first word of knowledge about her condition and did not understand the second word. Then how did she get healed? It was either God's sovereignty or the faith of her parents that caused this healing.

If you ask me, I believe it was the faith of her parents and not God's sovereignty alone that healed her. If she had been healed by God's sovereignty alone, then why had God not healed her before? Why would He wait fourteen years to heal this girl on this random night? I believe that as those parents saw and heard the testimony of Jesus, watched the videos of people who were healed and heard the preaching of the Word of God, it stirred faith in their hearts and they believed in a miracle for their daughter. I believe it was their faith that brought their daughter's healing into existence.

I also believe that like those parents who heard the words of knowledge and had their faith strengthened, as you read the testimonies and teachings in this book, your faith will be strengthened to the point where you will bring your healing—and the healing of those whom you pray for—into existence. The Bible says that creation is waiting for the manifestation of the children of God (see Romans 8:19). We are the ones who are supposed to destroy the works of the devil. We are the ones who are supposed to realize by faith the things of God that are not yet in existence (see Hebrews 11:1).

Watch Out for the Lies

Have you ever heard that "love will find a way"? God is love, and God will find a way. God is for you. He loves you and wants you healed and blessed in every area of your life. One of the greatest lies of the enemy—his greatest tool to prevent God's children from receiving their healing—is the belief that it is God's will for someone to be sick. But as Jesus said, "The thief comes only to steal and kill and destroy. I came that they may have life and have it abundantly" (John 10:10 ESV).

The devil is very slick. He does not come straight at you with a lie. As he did in the Garden, he distorts truth. He comes to you with questions: *Isn't God all-powerful? Can't God do anything? Is there anything impossible for God?* While these questions are harmless in themselves, the objective behind them is to get you to reason in your mind against the Word. For all these questions, our brains immediately come up with answers based on our own understanding.

If you lean on your own understanding, before too long you can find yourself in a dialogue with the serpent, the devil. Have you ever wondered why the serpent has a forked tongue? His tongue brings division. His words come to divide your mind, confuse you and lead you away from God. When you apply these questions with your own reasoning power to a situation where you are sick (or another person is sick), the answer that all things are possible for God (which is true) only leads you to one possible outcome:

God can do all things + God can heal any disease = God can heal me

God can heal me + I am still sick = God wants me to be sick

We might not admit to this line of reasoning, but when we do the math, we end up convincing ourselves that it is God's will for us (or someone else) to be sick. Then our minds come up with some terribly incorrect answers: *God is using this sickness to strengthen my faith. God is making me weak so He can be strong. Paul had a "thorn in the flesh," so this sickness must be my thorn.*

A Thorn in the Flesh

Before we go any further, let's talk about that idea of a "thorn in the flesh." Many people assume that a persistent condition or illness is a thorn in the flesh God has sent their way to better their character. Many Christians fall into this theological ditch. It is based on a common misunderstanding of Scripture. Here is the text people refer to that uses the term *thorn in the flesh*: "By reason of the exceeding greatness of the revelations, that I should not be exalted excessively, there was given to me a thorn in the flesh" (2 Corinthians 12:7 WEB).

This is the misunderstood passage written by the apostle Paul and used, or more accurately, misused by Christians to justify almost anything that goes wrong in their lives. The problem with that is that most people attribute their "thorn in the flesh" to God and think it is something He sent. This is the opposite of the truth—that God is the only one who can bring a solution to your problem. If you believe God sent your problem to you, then you will not come against God by fighting it. You will believe that you are being a good and submissive servant of the Lord by *not* fighting it, when, in fact, God had nothing to do with your so-called thorn in the flesh.

To solve the misunderstanding, let's look at the entire verse that phrase comes from: "By reason of the exceeding greatness of the revelations, that I should not be exalted excessively, there was given to me a thorn in the flesh, *a messenger of Satan to torment me*, that I should not be exalted excessively" (italics added). From that verse and other Scriptures, here is why it is incorrect to say that a persisting sickness or illness is from God:

1. *Paul's thorn in the flesh was not sickness.* Paul was not sick, as many assume. If he were sick, he would have used the word *sickness* in the Greek, *astheneo.* In fact, he did use *astheneo* to say that Epaphroditus and Trophimus were sick (see Philippians 2:25–26; 2 Timothy 4:20). If "thorn in the flesh" were an expression used to refer to sickness, Paul also would have said that these two men who were ill had a thorn in the flesh.

2. *The thorn was not sent by God.* Paul states that he asked three times to be delivered from his thorn in the flesh, but God did not intervene, saying instead that His grace was enough (see 2 Corinthians 12:8–9). Many people interpret Paul's declaration here to mean that the thorn was sent by God to keep him humble. Nevertheless, Paul had already clearly stated that the thorn in the flesh was sent by the devil, not by God (see verse 7).

3. *The thorn was not sent to humble Paul.* It is a misassumption to think that God allowed the thorn because He wanted to humble Paul. The Bible clearly shows that Paul was a humble man. Despite all his supernatural experiences with God, Paul kept his heart humble. His life was not his anymore; he had completely given it to Christ (see Philippians 1:21). When we humble ourselves, God exalts us (see 1 Peter 5:6). The devil was the one who sent the thorn to torment Paul, in an attempt to prevent the apostle from being exalted by God beyond measure.

4. *The thorn was a demon.* Paul makes it clear that his thorn was, as the apostle calls it, "a messenger of Satan." The

Greek word for *messenger* that Paul uses is *angelus,* which means angel, so Paul is saying that the thorn is an angel sent by the devil—in other words, a demon.

5. *The demon attacked Paul through persecution.* The Jews commonly used the expression "thorn in the flesh" to refer to persecution. The term only appears four times in the Old Testament, and in all these occurrences it refers to *persecution* (see Numbers 33:55; Joshua 23:13; Judges 2:2–3; Ezekiel 28:24). Was Paul suffering persecution? You bet! In Acts 13:49–50, we see that the Jews stirred up the city and raised persecution against Paul. In Acts 14:1–2, the unbelieving Jews stirred up the Gentiles against the brothers, of whom Paul was a leader. In Acts 14:19, the Jews persuaded the people to stone Paul and drag him outside the city, leaving him for dead. In Acts 17:5 and 17:13, the Jews stirred up the people against Paul. In Acts 19, Demetrius the silversmith opposed the apostle Paul and caused an uproar against him. In Acts 21:27–31, again the Jews tried to kill him. Are you convinced that Paul was suffering persecution? He was not a popular guy among the religious people who, deceived by the evil angel sent by the devil, persecuted Paul and continually tried to kill him.

What can we conclude from all this? When Paul asks the Lord to deliver him from his "thorn in the flesh," he is referring to a demonic spirit sent by the devil to stir up the religious people— mostly the unbelieving Jews, but also the Greeks—against his life and message. So the next time you hear someone say that he or she is sick, but it is okay because it is a thorn in the flesh sent by God, you are equipped to set the person free from this lie of the devil and point him or her in the direction where healing and miracles come from: God.

The Biggest Lie

This line of faulty reasoning that "God can heal me but hasn't, so it must be His will that I'm sick" is probably the biggest lie the devil uses to prevent God's children from receiving healing. Since he has no authority over your life, he uses your own power against you. Jesus said, "All authority in heaven and on earth has been given to me" (Matthew 28:18). How much authority was given to Jesus? That's right, all of it. If Jesus has all authority, then the devil has no authority over you. Then how does he attack you? He uses your own authority against you when you come into agreement with him.

As children of God we have power and authority over nature. The universe will come into alignment with whatever we believe and declare. (Remember the observer effect I talked about in chapter 4?) We bring things into existence by faith—that is, by believing. When you believe a lie, you empower that lie. That is how the devil works. He does not tell you a lie; he misleads you with truth out of context.

The truth is a powerful element in our world. The truth can set you free. The truth can empower you. The truth placed in the wrong context, however, will lead to your destruction. We see this clearly when Jesus was in the desert, being tempted by the devil:

> Then the devil took him to the holy city and had him stand on the highest point of the temple. "If you are the Son of God," he said, "throw yourself down. For it is written: 'He will command his angels concerning you, and they will lift you up in their hands, so that you will not strike your foot against a stone.'"
>
> Matthew 4:5–6

Here we see that the devil clearly is using truth, the Word, in his efforts to mislead Jesus. But Jesus knew exactly what game the devil was playing. He fought the devil's isolated truth with rightly contextualized truth when He answered, "It is also written: 'Do not put the Lord your God to the test'" (Matthew 4:7).

It is amazing how an isolated truth used in the wrong context can lead you astray from the truth. This is how the devil operated in the Garden, and this is how he tried to work with tempting Jesus. This is how he still works today. By quoting other Scriptures, what was Jesus doing? He was putting truth in the right context. This is why it is important for us to know the Word of God. We must do more than memorize verses. We must understand the Word, the very heart of God, by the Spirit of God.

Pressing In

Can God do all things? Yes, He can. Can God heal you? Yes, He can. Does the fact that you are still sick mean that sickness is God's will for you? The answer is a resounding "No!"

I want to prove that by using a couple of fictional conversations between me and two other interesting people: blind Bartimaeus and the Syrophoenician woman, both of whom sought out miracles from Jesus. The first conversation would go something like this:

"*Shalom*, Bartimaeus. How are you doing?" I say, walking up to him.

"Peace be unto you, foreigner. I'm doing all right. Have you any alms to bless me with?"

"No, sorry, I don't. I do have a strong impression that soon you won't be needing alms anymore."

"Oh yes? Why is that?"

"Well, I heard Jesus of Nazareth is coming this way."

"Really? When?"

"He should be here any minute now. Before He comes, I have a question for you. Do you believe God can do all things?"

"Yes, of course!"

"Do you believe God can heal you?"

"Sure, all things are possible for God."

"So, if all things are possible for God and He can heal you, yet you are still blind, don't you think that it's God's will for you to stay blind?"

"No, of course not. That's nonsense!"

"Well, how come?"

"Because God is good. He is love. My blindness did not come from Him. He is the Father of lights, and only good things come from Him. It is written that God will send the Christ, and He will restore the eyes of the blind. I believe the Christ is Jesus of Nazareth. Now, if you will excuse me, I can hear a crowd approaching. It's probably Jesus coming this way, so I'd better get ready, because I'm about to get my sight back."

Even though this is just an imaginary conversation, it is a very plausible one. When the disciples tried to convince Bartimaeus to stop shouting at Jesus, they could not. In fact, he cried out for Jesus all the more, such was his determination to get his healing (see Mark 10:46–52).

Now, let's look at another fictional dialogue between me and the Syrophoenician woman:

"Jesus! Have mercy on me, Lord!" the Syrophoenician woman cries to the Lord as He walks by her.

"Hello, madam . . ." Peter, who had been silent, finally speaks to her. "We're terribly sorry, but the Master is busy at the moment."

She seems to ignore Peter's presence and shouts over his shoulder, "Jesus, Son of David, have mercy on me! My daughter is demon-possessed."

At this point I step out of my invisible time machine and walk toward the woman, fixing the Israeli garment I rented from a local store near my home.

"Excuse me, madam," I say, "but why are you bothering the Master?"

"Because He can set my daughter free," she answers, her eyes still fixed on Jesus.

"But aren't you Greek? I thought that Greeks were polytheists," I say, fixing my fake mustache.

"I have no faith in the Greek pantheon of gods anymore," she says. "I have asked and continually prayed for them to heal my daughter, yet she remains sick and oppressed. When word of the deeds of Jesus of Nazareth reached our distant shores, I knew He was the Christ, the Anointed One, the God of the Jews. I believe He can heal my daughter."

"Do you believe God is good?"

"Yes, I do."

"Do you believe all things are possible for God?"

"Of course. He is the all-powerful God of the Jews, who took them out of Egypt with a mighty hand."

"So if God is good and can do all things and your daughter is still afflicted, then don't you think that it's God's will for her to be that way?"

"Of course not! Evil is all around us, but it doesn't come from God. God is good. My daughter isn't healed yet because God chose to operate His signs, wonders and miracles through His children. She will be oppressed until an anointed child of God comes to destroy the work of the devil in her life. This is how God chooses to set the captives free—through the hands of His sons and daughters. God operates through His children. An evil spirit afflicts her. It often attacks her and tries to kill her. This evil comes from the devil, but Jesus is the Son of God. I know He can heal my daughter. Now, if you will excuse me, I have a healing to claim."

You know the rest of the story. This woman, like many who came to Jesus, got her miracle by pressing in (see Matthew 15:21–28).

Or consider the man who could not walk and sat by the pool, waiting for the angel to stir up the waters (see John 5:2–9). Even though for thirty-eight years he did not get his healing, he never gave up hope. Thirty-eight years is a long time to wait for a miracle. I have seen many people give up and turn bitter against God after thirty-eight minutes, let alone thirty-eight weeks, months or years. Yes, it took him a lifetime, but you know what? He got his healing!

Is it God's will for you to be sick? No, it is not. No matter how long it takes, no matter how hard you have to press in, believe and contend for your miracle and you will get it.

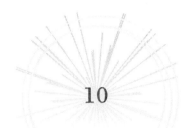

10

The Power of Belief

Jesus looked at them and said, "With man this is impossible, but with God all things are possible."

Matthew 19:26

It is interesting how most people whom Jesus healed in the New Testament were not concerned about theology. They were only concerned about getting healed. The time has come for us to stop trying to "figure things out" and start experiencing and enjoying the goodness of God.

Belief is a powerful weapon. It can be used for your benefit or your destruction. As I pointed out in the previous chapter, the devil wants to use your own faith against you, making you believe that whatever you are going through is God's will for your life. I tell you this: If whatever you are going through is not good and perfect, then it is not God's will for your life.

There is no mountain so high or valley so low that it can prevent God's goodness from reaching you. Only unbelief can do that, so fill your heart with faith. Change the way you think.

Understand that God wants only what is good and perfect for you, and press in for your miracle. Don't just sit there waiting and thinking, *Oh, if God wants to, He can heal me*. If Bartimaeus or the Syrophoenician woman thought like that, then they would not have received their miracles. They got what they wanted because they pushed through; they pressed in. Don't wait passively for God to touch you. Instead, boldly press in to touch Him.

Think of the woman with the issue of blood (see Matthew 9:20–22). Jesus didn't even know who she was until she pressed in and touched Him. Go to Him. Press in, boldly persist and believe for your miracle. What are you waiting for? It is time for you to claim your miracle. It is time for you to be healed and stay healed!

Faith, Fear and R-I-S-K

"Faith is taking the first step even when you do not see the whole staircase," Martin Luther King Jr. said. I love that phrase. Faith is taking a step even when you are not sure if your foot will find solid ground. Faith is the assurance of attaining what is expected even when there is no physical sign of what we hope for.

So it was with Peter. Even though a person cannot walk on water, Peter left the safety of the boat. The Sea of Galilee was rough the night that Jesus called him to walk on water, so much so that the wind and waves made Peter afraid and he began to sink. Fear is the opposite of faith. Fear is faith in evil. It is faith that something that can go wrong will go wrong. Fear is faith in Murphy's law. And if we believe that what can go wrong will go wrong, then the power of our faith begins to make the universe come into line with what we believe. This was the reason Peter started to sink, even though Jesus Himself had told him to come out of the boat and walk on water.

This is still true today. No matter how much God may want you to be healed, if you believe the lies of the devil instead of the truth of the Holy Spirit, you will *sink*. Don't put your faith in the storm around you. Don't pay any attention to the winds and waves that come to scare you away from your healing. Fear is inevitable. Naturally speaking, fear actually is a very important feeling. In the natural, fear keeps us from getting hurt by making us avoid dangerous and harmful situations. But spiritually speaking, fear is the opposite of faith. In the spiritual realm, fear and unbelief walk hand in hand. We must walk on the water of fear and unbelief, and not sink in it. Set your eyes on Jesus, and you will walk on water. If we put our faith and our eyes on Christ, He will give us our expected end.

As I mentioned earlier, John Wimber used to say that faith is spelled R-I-S-K. I also love that phrase, and I know it is true. Without risk you will never grow in your faith and your relationship with God. Take that step out of the boat, out of your comfort zone, and align your heart, mind and soul with God. In taking that step of faith, you will experience His good, pleasant and perfect will manifest in your life (see Romans 12:2).

Repeat Treatments

Some people give up on healing if nothing happens immediately after someone prays for them (or immediately after they pray for others). Yet these same people will follow a doctor's orders to the letter if he or she prescribes a treatment that consists of repeating the same medication several times a day. They don't complain about having to repeat the medication or even repeat the whole treatment in some cases. But when it comes to prayer for healing, they think it must be a onetime deal, and if nothing happens they believe it must be God's will that they are sick.

(Remember, we talked in chapter 9 about watching out for the enemy's lies in this area.)

Is it really God's will for these people not to be healed? Could it be that their healing is just around the corner and all they have to do is press in a little bit longer? Perhaps pray a few more times? Could it be that these people are believing it is not God's will for them to be healed, when in fact all it would take is a little more persistence and faith? I believe so.

There is nothing wrong with praying more than once. Even Jesus, on a certain occasion, had to pray more than once for the healing of a blind man (see Mark 8:22–26). I want to encourage you to pray for healing not only once, but as many times as necessary. Pray for healing as if you (or the person you are praying for) were going under a spiritual treatment prescribed by Dr. Jesus. Here is His prescription for you:

- Step 1: Lay hands on the part of your body (or the other person's) that needs healing. If it is inappropriate to lay hands on that specific body part, then lay hands on the shoulder. You may also use anointing oil if you like (see Mark 16:18; James 5:14).

- Step 2: Command the sickness to leave in the name and authority of Jesus. Don't just ask, using a prayer of petition, for the Father to heal if it is His will. I am telling you right now, *healing is the Father's will.* Come into agreement with the Holy Spirit, who dwells inside you, and use your authority as an heir of the Kingdom to command sickness to leave this body in Jesus' name (see Matthew 10:8).

- Step 3: Repeat steps 1 and 2 as many times as necessary, until the healing manifests or until the Holy Spirit tells you to stop praying. You must always be sensitive to the guidance of the Holy Spirit. If the person is not healed, encourage him or her to read the stories of the miracles of Jesus (see Appendix B) and to continue getting prayed for and believing for healing.

"Rejoice always, pray without ceasing, in everything give thanks; for this is the will of God in Christ Jesus for you" (1 Thessalonians 5:16–17 NKJV). I love this Scripture, which contains such a short yet powerful phrase: *pray without ceasing*. It speaks volumes to us. It is why you should follow step 3 *as many times as necessary*. The entire first epistle of Paul to the Thessalonians, which this passage comes out of, is a great blessing and encouragement to the Church. Paul had left Thessalonica by night to escape his persecutors. After staying there a shorter time than he had originally planned, he left behind new converts who had embraced his message and turned away from paganism (see Acts 17:1–10). Paul's purpose in writing this first letter was to encourage these new Thessalonian converts, giving them direction and instruction concerning how Christians should live a godly life. And in this short and simple phrase from that letter, Paul shares a powerful principle: Christians should not cease praying.

God Says Yes

I want to end this book with these final encouraging words: Do not give up your miracle. Do not cease to pray for yourself, as well as for others, for in Christ Jesus all God's promises for you are *yes* (see 2 Corinthians 1:20).

Today God says *yes* to you—*yes* to your healing, *yes* to your joy, *yes* to your deliverance, *yes* to your financial breakthrough, *yes* to your career, *yes* to happiness in your marriage, *yes* to the blessings you have been asking of Him for you and your loved ones.

I also trust that through reading these pages, you have seen that God says *yes*, you can *be healed and stay healed*. I hope that the practical tools and key principles about healing we looked at have helped you. I hope that the amazing testimonies I related from all over the world have built your faith. And I hope that the prayers I provided at the end of several chapters have shown you how to operate in words of command for healing and how to be thankful to God for every improvement. (Appendix A just ahead contains one more helpful prayer for you and some final words of encouragement as you seek healing for yourself and others.)

I trust you now know that *all God's promises for you are yes*, and that we, the Church, together declare, *"Amen!"*

Appendix A

Prayer for Healing

If you are suffering at any level, know that it is not the Father's will. He wants you whole. He wants you completely restored, whether it is in your hearing, your sight, your ability to walk or any other ability you should have that is being affected by an illness or affliction in your body or soul. I would like us to pray together for your healing. I have faith that you can receive your healing right now in Jesus' name. If you have faith to be healed, please pray this prayer with me:

Heavenly Father, thank You for Your love and grace. Thank You for sending Your Son, Jesus, to die for me on the cross. Jesus, thank You for the price You paid for me and for letting Your body be broken so that mine could be whole. Fill me with Your love. Come, Holy Spirit, and fill me. Give me a new passion for You, Lord.

Because there is no sickness or infirmity in heaven, I know that it is not Your will for there to be any sickness on earth. Thank You for being so good to me, Father. I love You.

Now, if it is convenient, place your hand where your infirmity is and say this:

In the name and authority of Jesus, I rebuke any sickness or affliction in my body. I command it to leave now in Jesus' name! Leave now and never come back. I bless my body, and I command every molecule, bone, ligament and organ in my body to be made whole, to be blessed and healed and to line up with God's will for my life. I decree and declare my blessing. Come, Holy Spirit, release Your blessing. I come into agreement with the Father's good and perfect will for my life, and I receive my healing in Jesus' name!

Remember that after praying, it is important to test your body for signs of healing. Try to do something you could not do before the prayer. Many people are healed as they take this step of faith. If you prayed to be healed of deafness, go ahead and snap your fingers next to your ears to see if there is any improvement. If you prayed for your eyes, try reading something you could not read before. If you had a muscular or skeletal problem, move your body and test it to see if you are any better.

If you notice any improvement, be grateful to God and take it as a sign that you are being healed. Remember that a spirit of thanksgiving increases the anointing. God loves a grateful heart, so be thankful for every little sign of healing. Once healing takes place, share your testimony. Give Him praise by telling others what He has done for you.

If you did not get your healing yet, be patient. Worship God and meditate on His promises for healing. Listen to testimonies that will build your faith, and keep a peaceful heart.

Be persistent! Don't lose heart if you don't see an immediate change. Even Jesus had to pray for a blind man twice. Continue to come into agreement with the Word of God, and the day will come when you also will be healed and stay healed in Jesus' name!

Appendix B

The Miracles of Jesus

Healing by Command

What: Water into wine
Reference: John 2:1–11 NKJV
Command: "Fill the waterpots with water. . . . Draw some out now."

What: Nobleman's son healed
Reference: John 4:46–54
Command: "Go; your son will live."

What: First miraculous provision of fish
Reference: Luke 5:1–11
Command: "Put out into the deep water, and let down the nets for a catch."

What: Leper healed
Reference: Matthew 8:2–4; Mark 1:40–45; Luke 5:12–15
Command: "I am willing. . . . Be clean!"

What: Centurion's servant healed
Reference: Matthew 8:5–13; Luke 7:1–10
Command: "Go! Let it be done just as you believed it would."

What: Widow's son raised to life
Reference: Luke 7:11–17
Command: "Young man, I say to you, get up!"

What: Peter's mother-in-law healed
Reference: Matthew 8:14–15; Mark 1:29–31; Luke 4:38–39
Command: "He touched her hand and the fever left her."

What: Paralytics healed
Reference: Matthew 9:2–8; Mark 2:1–12; Luke 5:17–26; John 5:1–16
Command: "Get up, take your mat and go home."

What: Man with withered hand healed
Reference: Matthew 12:10–14; Mark 3:1–6; Luke 6:6–11
Command: "Stretch out your hand."

What: Blind and dumb man healed after deliverance
Reference: Matthew 12:22–24; Luke 11:14
Command: "Jesus was driving out a demon that was mute. When the demon left, the man who had been mute spoke." (We can assume the command here was "come out," as Jesus also said in Mark 1:25.)

What: Tempest stilled
Reference: Matthew 8:23–27; Mark 4:35–41; Luke 8:22–25
Command: "He got up and rebuked the winds and the waves; and it was completely calm."

What: Demon dispossessed in Gadara
Reference: Matthew 8:28–34; Mark 5:1–20
Command: "Go!"

What: Jairus's daughter raised to life
Reference: Matthew 9:18–26; Mark 5:22–43; Luke 8:41–56
Command: "He went in and took the girl by the hand, and she got up."

What: Woman's issue of blood healed
Reference: Matthew 9:20–22 ESV; Mark 5:25–34; Luke 8:43–48
Command: "Take heart, daughter; your faith has made you well."

What: Two blind men restored to sight
Reference: Matthew 9:27–31
Command: "According to your faith let it be done to you."

What: Dumb demoniac healed
Reference: Matthew 9:32–34
Command: "When the demon was driven out, the man who had been mute spoke."

What: Five thousand miraculously fed
Reference: Matthew 14:13–21; Mark 6:31–44; Luke 9:10–17; John 6:5–14
Command: "Taking the five loaves and the two fish . . . he gave thanks and broke the loaves. Then he gave them to the disciples, and the disciples gave them to the people."

What: Jesus walks on the sea
Reference: Matthew 14:22–33 ESV; Mark 6:45–52; John 6:16–21
Command: "He said, 'Come.' So Peter got out of the boat and walked on the water and came to Jesus."

What: Syrophoenician's daughter healed
Reference: Matthew 15:21–28; Mark 7:24–30
Command: "Woman, you have great faith! Your request is granted."

What: Deaf and dumb man healed
Reference: Mark 7:31–37 ESV
Command: "'Ephphatha,' that is, 'Be opened.'"

What: Four thousand fed
Reference: Matthew 15:32–39; Mark 8:1–9
Command: "When he had given thanks, be broke them and gave them to the disciples, and they in turn to the people."

What: Blind man restored to sight
Reference: Mark 8:22–26 NRSV
Command: "When he had put saliva on his eyes and laid his hands on him, he asked him, 'Can you see anything?' And the man looked up and said, 'I can see people, but they look like trees, walking.'

Then Jesus laid his hands on his eyes again; and he looked intently and his sight was restored."

What: Demoniac and lunatic boy healed
Reference: Matthew 17:14–21 NRSV; Mark 9:14–29; Luke 9:37–43
Command: "Jesus rebuked the demon, and it came out of him, and the boy was cured instantly."

What: Miraculous provision of tribute
Reference: Matthew 17:24–27 NKJV
Command: "Go to the sea, cast in a hook, and take the fish that comes up first. And when you have opened its mouth, you will find a piece of money; take that and give it to them for Me and you."

What: The eyes of one born blind opened
Reference: John 9:1–41
Command: "Go . . . wash in the pool of Siloam."

What: Woman cured of an eighteen-year infirmity
Reference: Luke 13:10–17
Command: "Woman, you are set free from your infirmity."

What: Dropsical man (swelling disorder) healed
Reference: Luke 14:1–6
Command: "So taking hold of the man, he healed him and sent him on his way."

What: Ten lepers cleansed
Reference: Luke 17:11–19
Command: "Go, show yourselves to the priests."

What: Lazarus raised to life
Reference: John 11:1–46
Command: "Lazarus, come out!"

What: Blind beggar restored to sight
Reference: Mark 10:46–52; Luke 18:35–43
Command: "Go . . . your faith has healed you."

What: Barren fig tree blighted
Reference: Matthew 21:18–19; Mark 11:12–24
Command: "May no one ever eat fruit from you again."

What: Malchus's ear healed
Reference: Matthew 26:51–56; Mark 14:47–49; Luke 22:50–51; John 18:10–11
Command: "But Jesus answered, 'No more of this!' And he touched the man's ear and healed him."

What: Second provision of fish
Reference: John 21:1–14
Command: "Throw your net on the right side of the boat and you will find some."

Appendix C

The Miracles of the Disciples

Healing by Command

What: Anointing with oil many who were sick
Reference: Mark 6:13
Command: "They drove out many demons and anointed many sick people with oil and healed them."

What: Preaching and healing everywhere
Reference: Luke 9:6
Command: "So they set out and went from village to village, proclaiming the good news and healing people everywhere."

What: Preaching everywhere, with signs following
Reference: Mark 16:20
Command: "The disciples went out and preached everywhere, and the Lord worked with them and confirmed his word by the signs that accompanied it."

What: Lame man healed
Reference: Acts 3:1–16
Command: "In the name of Jesus Christ of Nazareth, walk."

What: Sick in the streets healed
Reference: Acts 5:15
Command: "People brought the sick into the streets and laid them on beds and mats so that at least Peter's shadow might fall on some of them as he passed by."

What: Stephen's great wonders and miracles
Reference: Acts 6:8
Command: "Stephen . . . performed great wonders and signs among the people."

What: Philip's miracles at Samaria
Reference: Acts 8:5–8
Command: "With shrieks, impure spirits came out of many, and many who were paralyzed or lame were healed."

What: Aeneas, who had been bedridden eight years and was paralyzed, healed
Reference: Acts 9:33–34
Command: "Aeneas . . . Jesus Christ heals you. Get up and roll up your mat."

What: Girl raised from the dead
Reference: Acts 9:36–40 NRSV
Command: "He turned to the body and said, 'Tabitha, get up.'"

What: Brother Ananias lays hands on Saul of Tarsus
Reference: Acts 9:17–18 NRSV
Command: "He laid his hands on Saul and said, 'Brother Saul, the Lord Jesus, who appeared to you on your way here, has sent me so that you may regain your sight and be filled with the Holy Spirit.'"
The text here does not say how Ananias prayed, but it shows us that he did not ask the Father to heal Saul of the scales on his eyes. Ananias declares that Jesus sent him *so that* Saul could regain his sight. We can reasonably assume that Ananias prayed a prayer of command, as every other disciple in the book of Acts did, commanding the scales to fall off. That is a reasonable guess, but even if some would disagree, the fact remains that this prayer was not a prayer of petition. Ananias communicated to Paul what Jesus

had told him to do, and the next verse says, "And immediately something like scales fell from his eyes."

What: Signs and wonders at Iconium
Reference: Acts 14:3
Command: "The Lord . . . confirmed the message of his grace by enabling them to perform signs and wonders."

What: Crippled man healed
Reference: Acts 14:8–10
Command: "'Stand up on your feet!' At that, the man jumped up and began to walk."

What: Unusual miracles by the hands of Paul
Reference: Acts 19:11–12 NLT
Command: "God gave Paul the power to perform unusual miracles. When handkerchiefs or aprons that had merely touched his skin were placed on sick people, they were healed of their diseases, and evil spirits were expelled." Again, there are no prayers of petition here. People learned through the testimony of the woman healed of the issue of blood that if they touched the clothes of an anointed one, they would be healed. That word spread among the believers like fire on dry stubble. They would now pick up Paul's aprons and handkerchiefs and touch the sick with them, in faith, and the sick would be healed. No prayer was said in cases like this; it was a declaration of faith like the woman with the issue of blood made: "For she thought to herself, 'If I can just touch his robe, I will be healed.' Immediately the bleeding stopped, and she could feel in her body that she had been healed of her terrible condition" (Mark 5:28–29 NLT). Notice that she did not pray and ask for her healing. She determined, decreed and declared in her heart that if she only touched His garments she would be healed, and so she was. We can assume that the cases Acts 19:11–12 refers to followed that principle. That woman and other believers who learned the principle also applied it, and they got their healings not by asking, but by determining in their hearts that it would be so.

What: Eutychus's life restored
Reference: Acts 20:9–12
Command: "Don't be alarmed," he said. "He's alive!"

What: Publius's father healed
Reference: Acts 28:7–8
Command: "Paul went in to see him and, after prayer, placed his hands on him and healed him."

What: Sick people healed
Reference: Acts 28:9
Command: "The rest of the sick on the island came and were cured."

Notes

Chapter 1: The Deaf Hear: Be Motivated by Love

1. "Stem Cell Therapy," Stanford School of Medicine, accessed September 24, 2015, https://hearinglosscure.stanford.edu/stem-cell-therapy.

Chapter 4: The Lepers Are Cleansed: Words of Command

1. For more information on the laying on of hands, read Randy Clark's book on impartation, *There Is More! The Secret to Experiencing God's Power to Change Your Life* (Chosen Books, 2013).

2. If you want to know more about this important subject, I highly recommend Don Gossett's book *What You Say Is What You Get!* (Whitaker House, 1976).

3. Fred Alan Wolfe, "Awakening your Soul or: Becoming aware that you are a Spiritual Universe," FredAlanWolf.com, accessed September 24, 2015, http://www.fredalanwolf.com/myarticles/awakening%20your%20soul.pdf.

Chapter 5: The Dead Are Raised: Atmospheres of Faith

1. Bill O'Reilly and Martin Dugard, *Killing Jesus: A History* (New York: Henry Holt & Co., 2013), 91.

Chapter 6: Miracles

1. *Oxford Learner's Dictionaries*, s.v. "healing," accessed June 1, 2015, http://www.oxfordlearnersdictionaries.com/us/definition/english/healing.

2. Ibid., s.v. "miracle," accessed June 1, 2015, http://www.oxfordlearnersdictionaries.com/us/definition/english/miracle.

3. Julian Wilson, *Wigglesworth: The Complete Story* (Milton Keynes: Authentic Media, 2004), 82–83.

Chapter 8: Demonic Affliction

1. These *favelas* (slums) first appeared in Brazil in the late nineteenth century and were built by former slaves and their descendants, who did not have the means to own any land. Once these slaves gained their freedom, many of them moved closer to the big cities to find work. Besides former slaves, many others also came from rural areas to live in the *favelas* while they tried to find work in the fast-growing cities of Rio de Janeiro and São Paulo (where most of the *favelas* are located). The inhabitants would build shacks next to each other that were meant to be temporary homes. Due to the lack of any kind of control from the government, however, they ended up becoming permanent homes for thousands of families.

2. For more information about deliverance, I recommend Pablo Bottari's book *Free in Christ: Your Complete Handbook on the Ministry of Deliverance* (Charisma House, 2000). Also see Randy Clark's *Ministry Team Training Manual* (Apostolic Network of Global Awakening, 2012), specifically the chapter on ten steps for deliverance.

Chapter 9: Believe the Word

1. For a detailed study on words of knowledge, please refer to Randy Clark's *Ministry Team Training Manual* (Apostolic Network of Global Awakening, 2012), which is available at www.globalawakening.com.

Ed Rocha graduated from the International Bible Institute of London and is currently pursuing his master's degree in theology. During his time in London, Ed received a strong impartation and experienced the Holy Spirit in a powerful way. This prophetic encounter prepared him to receive a direct impartation for the healing ministry from Randy Clark, Ed's spiritual mentor and father, in 2005.

After this impartation, Ed began to see healings, signs and wonders flow in his life and ministry. Today Ed ministers all over Brazil, North America and Europe. His revival meetings are marked by a strong presence of God, words of knowledge, healings and powerful impartations.

Ed and his wife, Dani, live in Rio de Janeiro, Brazil, where they are planting a church under the Global Awakening Network.

For more information about Ed Rocha and his ministries, please visit www.edrocha.org. Also, whatever illness you may have had, if you were healed at any point as you were reading this book, Ed would like to hear about it so that he can rejoice and celebrate your healing with you. Please send your testimony to info@edrocha.org.